THE SERVANT OF JEHOVAH

THE SERVANT OF JEHOVAH:

THE SUFFERINGS OF THE MESSIAH AND THE GLORY THAT SHOULD FOLLOW

AN EXPOSITION OF ISAIAH LIII

by DAVID BARON

LONDON
MARSHALL, MORGAN & SCOTT
EDINBURGH

MARSHALL, MORGAN AND SCOTT, LTD.
33 LUDGATE HILL, LONDON, E.C.4

U.S.A.
ZONDERVAN PUBLISHING HOUSE
847 OTTAWA AVENUE, N.W.
GRAND RAPIDS
MICHIGAN

First Edition . . . . *January 1922*
Second Edition . . . *October 1922*
New Edition . . . . *Spring 1954*
Reprinted . . . . . *October 1954*

MADE AND PRINTED IN GREAT BRITAIN BY
MORRISON AND GIBB LIMITED, LONDON AND EDINBURGH

INTRODUCTION TO NEW EDITION

No greater service has been rendered to the Christian public during the past few years than the republishing of David Baron's works. David Baron was not only an unusually able and consecrated missionary to his people—the Jews—but he was a spiritual giant, mighty in the Scriptures. He brought to his task the rare and happy combination of keen spiritual insight and sane and sanctified scholarship.

In these days when Jewish leaders, as a defence against Christianity, are trying to eliminate from the pages of the Old Testament the doctrine of a personal Messiah, and so, in reality, undermining the very foundations of true Judaism, and " liberal " writers within the " Church " are devoted to the same purpose, it is a source of genuine satisfaction and strength to the cause of Christ in general and to Jewish Evangelism in particular that such a work as *The Servant of Jehovah* should again be made available to the public.

Thoroughly steeped in Rabbinic lore and literature and the polemics of Judaism, no one was better able to expose the fallacies of the more modern Jewish interpretation of this great and sublime portion of the Old Testament, Isaiah liii., which has been aptly referred to as " the bad conscience of the Synagogue."

But David Baron's purpose in the writing of this book was not only the critical and controversial but the continuous exposition of this greatest of all prophetic utterances, to convince of its truth and to strengthen faith, so that like Philip of old when one came to him concerning this passage asking " of whom speaketh the prophet this ? " we may be better able to preach unto them Jesus (Acts viii. 34). And the reader will realize a spiritual exaltation through the reading of this rich exposition, and a fuller comprehension of the meaning of the glorious atonement accomplished by " The Servant of Jehovah," Israel's promised Redeemer.

PREFACE

It is, I can sincerely say, with unfeigned diffidence that I send forth this little work on its mission, for I am deeply conscious of the greatness and sublimity of the theme and of the inadequate way in which I have been able to deal with it. I felt inwardly impelled to write it, and have gladly devoted to it what days and hours could possibly be spared in a life of strain and pressure on account of many other tasks and responsibilities.

But though sensible of the shortcoming and imperfection of my effort, I have the heart assurance that there is a blessing in it, and if the reader receives only a fraction of the spiritual help and enjoyment which the writer found in the course of his meditation and exposition of this truly wonderful Scripture he will be amply rewarded. It has confirmed his faith in the supernatural character of prophecy and made him feel as never before that Holy Scripture has upon it "the stamp of its Divine Author—the mark of heaven—the impress of eternity."

It has, if possible, wrought deeper conviction in his heart that Jesus of Nazareth is indeed the Christ, the promised Redeemer of Israel—He "of whom Moses in the law and the prophets did write"; for it is beyond even the wildest credulity to believe that the resemblance in every feature and minutest detail between this prophetic portraiture drawn centuries before His advent and the story of His life, and death, and glorious resurrection as narrated in the Gospels, can be mere accident or fortuitous coincidence. It has also strengthened my hope for the future blessing of the nation from which I have sprung, and for which I have not ceased to yearn with the yearnings of Him who wept over Jerusalem, and even on the Cross prayed for them : "Father, forgive them, for they know not what they do"; for, in the words of Franz Delitzsch, " we must not overlook the fact that this golden passional is also one of the greatest prophecies of the future conversion of the nation which has rejected the Servant of God, and allowed the Gentiles to be the first to recognize Him. At last, though very late, it will feel remorse. And when this shall once take place, then, and not till then, will this chapter—which, to use an old epithet, will ever be *carnificina Rabbinorum*—receive its complete historical fulfilment."

As will be seen, the book consists of two parts. In the first part it has been impossible to avoid controversy and criticism in order to clear the ground, and to demonstrate the firm foundation on which the Messianic interpretation of the prophecies concerning the Servant of Jehovah in the Book of Isaiah is based; while in the second part, which is a continuous exposition of the great Scripture which forms the subject of the whole,

I have tried as much as possible to avoid controversy and criticism, but to make it *spiritually helpful* to believers.

There is nothing in these pages which should be too difficult or abstruse for the ordinary intelligent reader who knows no other language than English; the Hebrew words and phrases where they occur being all transliterated as well as translated. To those, however, who have no interest in the history of interpretation, and do not care to follow Jewish and rationalistic misinterpretations, I would recommend to read the exposition first, or to pass over Chapters II. and III. of the first part.

DAVID BARON.

CONTENTS

PART I

A CRITICAL EXAMINATION OF THE NON-MESSIANIC INTERPRETATIONS OF ISAIAH LIII.

PART II

THE EXPOSITION

THE SCRIPTURE

BEHOLD, My Servant shall deal wisely, He shall be exalted and lifted up, and shall be very high.

Like as many were astonished at Thee : (His visage was so marred more than any man, and His form more than the sons of men),

So shall He sprinkle many nations ; kings shall shut their mouths at Him : for that which had not been told them shall they see ; and that which they had not heard shall they understand.

Who hath believed our message? and to whom hath the arm of Jehovah been revealed?

For He grew up before Him as a tender plant, and as a root out of a dry ground. He hath no form nor comeliness ; and when we see Him, there is no beauty that we should desire Him.

He was despised, and rejected of men ; a man of sorrows, and acquainted with grief : and as one from whom men hide their face He was despised and we esteemed Him not.

Surely He hath borne our griefs, and carried our sorrows : yet we did esteem Him stricken, smitten of God, and afflicted.

But He was wounded for our transgressions. He was bruised for our iniquities : the chastisement of our peace was upon Him ; and with His stripes we are healed.

All we like sheep have gone astray ; we have turned every one to his own way, and Jehovah hath laid on Him the iniquity of us all.

He was oppressed, yet when He was afflicted He opened not His mouth ; as a lamb that is led to the slaughter, and as a sheep that before its shearers is dumb, so He opened not His mouth.

By oppression and judgment He was taken away ; and as for His generation, who among them considered that He was cut off out of the land of the living for the transgression of My people to whom the stroke was due?

And they made His grave with the wicked, and with a rich man in His death ; although He had done no violence neither was any deceit in His mouth.

Yet it pleased Jehovah to bruise Him ; He hath put Him to grief : when Thou shalt make His soul an offering for sin, He shall see His seed, He shall prolong His days, and the pleasure of the Lord shall prosper in His hands.

He shall see of the travail of His soul, and shall be satisfied : by the knowledge of Himself shall My righteous Servant justify many ; and He shall bear their iniquities.

Therefore will I divide Him a portion with the great, and He shall divide the spoil with the strong ; because He poured out His soul unto death, and was numbered with the transgressors : yet He bare the sin of many, and made intercession for the transgressors.

[*Translation of the American " Standard Edition."*]

PART I

A CRITICAL EXAMINATION OF THE NON-MESSIANIC INTERPRETATIONS OF ISAIAH LIII.

"I pray thee, of whom speaketh the prophet this? of himself, or of some other?"—ACTS viii. 34.

CHAPTER I

THE PROPHETIC GEM AND ITS SETTING

THE great Scripture we are about to consider has sometimes been called "the fifth Gospel." "Methinks," said
Augustine, "Isaiah writes not a prophecy but a gospel."
This he said of the whole book, but it is especially true
of this chapter. Polycarp, the disciple of John, called
it "the golden Passional of the Old Testament"; and a
great German scholar writes: "It looks as if it had been
written beneath the cross of Golgotha and was illuminated
by the heavenly brightness of the שֵׁב לִימִינִי, *shebh limini*
('Sit Thou at My right hand'). It is the unravelling of
Psalms xxii. and cx. It forms the inmost centre of this
wonderful book of consolations (as the Rabbis called the
second half of Isaiah), and is the most central, the deepest, and the loftiest thing that Old Testament prophecy,
outstripping itself, has ever achieved." Luther said that
every Christian ought to be able to repeat it by heart.

"It is prelude to much that is most distinctive in New
Testament doctrine, and is the root from which not a
little of the thinking of Christian ages has grown. Its
phraseology has entered largely into Christian speech,

and it has supplied more texts to the gospel preacher
than any other portion of the Old Testament.   There
are individual phrases in it resembling peaks, from which
we faintly descry vast realms of truth which we cannot
yet explore, but which shine with a mystic light whose
source is Divine.   Beyond question, this chapter is the
heart of the Hebrew prophetic writings.   It embraces
and harmonizes the ideas contained in such seemingly
discordant predictions as Psalms ii., xxii., lxxii., and cx. ;
and from the standpoint which it furnishes we are enabled
to see the consistency of Messianic prophecy throughout.

"Elsewhere, indeed, we find greater splendour of
language, force of passion, wealth of imagery, and imagi-
native elevation, but nowhere so full, minute, and vivid
forthshowing of God's purpose.   Truths elsewhere seen
in twilight and transitory glimpses here stand forth
for calm inspection in the light of day.   Elsewhere we
find line or touch or feature in keeping with what is here ;
but nowhere so finished and complete a portraiture.   It
is as if the prophet had shaded and filled up with colours
the outlines elsewhere given.   The hints of One passing
through shame and suffering to victory, which elsewhere
appear as 'dark sayings,' here kindle into a great life-
filled picture, in which we see not only His surpassing
sorrow, but also the mystery of its meaning, and the
glory which finally comes of it.   Not merely is there
broad outline, but those more delicate lines and contours
which give perfect individuality to the portrait.

" The chapter holds much the same place in Old Testament prophecy that the narrative of Christ's death, burial, and resurrection holds in New Testament history; and with this chapter all Hebrew prophecy as a Divine thing stands or falls." [1]

But most precious and beautiful as this Old Testament prophetic gem is in itself, its lustre is greatly intensified by its setting.

The second half of the Book of Isaiah, consisting of the last twenty-seven chapters, is the sublimest and richest portion of Old Testament revelation. It forms a single continuous prophecy which occupies the same position in the prophetic Scriptures as the Book of Deuteronomy in the Pentateuch, and the Gospel of John in relation to the Synoptic Gospels. It is true that "it does not flow on in even current like a history," and to the superficial reader it may have a desultory appearance, but "after patient study the first sense of confusedness is got over, and we perceive its magnificent and harmonious completeness as it rounds itself into one glorious vision."

It may be called the prophetic Messianic epic of the Old Testament. It is sublime in its very style and language, and wonderful in its comprehensiveness—anticipating, as it does, the whole order of the New Testament. It begins, where the New Testament begins, with the ministry of John the Baptist—"the voice of

---

[1] *The Man of Sorrows and the Joy that was Set before Him*— a very excellent booklet by the late James Culross, D.D., published by the Drummond Tract Depository, to which I shall have occasion to make many references in the exposition.

him that crieth in the wilderness, Prepare ye the way of the Lord," and it ends, where the New Testament ends, with the new heavens and a new earth, wherein shall dwell righteousness.[1]

On examining the glorious prophecy closely, we find that the twenty-seven chapters range themselves into three equal divisions of nine chapters each, all ending with nearly the same solemn refrain, " There is no peace, saith my God, to the wicked."[2]

One great line of thought unfolded in the whole prophecy is the development of evil and the final overthrow of the wicked, who are excluded from the blessings of Messiah's Kingdom ; and the sufferings but final glory of the righteous remnant, who are the subjects of that Kingdom, and whose King is described as leading the way along the same path of suffering into glory.

This subject becomes developed and intensified as we go on, until it reaches its climax in the last chapter.

The first section is brought to a close at the end of chapter xlviii., where the blessedness of the righteous who are "redeemed" (ver. 20), and peacefully led and satisfied even in the desert, is contrasted with the state of the wicked to whom "there is no peace."

In the second division the same subject becomes intensified ; there is development of both evil and good, righteousness and wickedness, and it ends with chapter lvii., where " Peace ! peace !" is announced to the

---

[1] Chaps. lxv. 17–20, lxvi. 22.

[2] Chaps. xlviii. 22, lvii. 21, lxvi. 24.

righteous, but the wicked have not only "no peace," but have become "like the troubled sea when it cannot rest, whose waters cast up mire and dirt."

In the last division the destiny of both is brought to a climax and becomes fixed for ever. "Therefore thus saith Jehovah God, Behold, My servants shall eat, but ye shall be hungry; behold, My servants shall drink, but ye shall be thirsty; behold, My servants shall rejoice, but ye shall be ashamed; behold, My servants shall sing for joy, but ye shall cry for sorrow of heart and shall howl for vexation of spirit. And ye shall leave your name for a curse unto My chosen, for the Lord God shall slay thee, and call His servants by another name." This contrast is continued until finally we find the righteous dwelling for ever in the new heavens and the new earth, wherein shall dwell righteousness; while as to the wicked who have transgressed against God, "their worm shall not die, neither shall their fire be quenched, and they shall be an abhorring to all flesh."

In the first section (chaps. xl.–xlviii.) the restoration from Babylon (which, however, is portrayed in terms which far exceeded what actually took place at that restoration, and which will only be exhaustively fulfilled in the greater restoration of Israel "from the four corners of the earth") is the starting-point, and the appointed instrument in God's hand to bring about that restoration, Cyrus, is the central figure.

In the second or central section (chaps. xlix.–lvii.) the grand redemption to be accomplished by One greater than Cyrus—even by Him, who in this series of chapters is pre-eminently the *Ebhed Yehovah* — the "Servant of Jehovah," who is sent not only to raise up "the tribes of Jacob," and to restore "the preserved of Israel," but to be "a light also to the Gentiles," and God's salvation "unto the end of the earth," is the theme with which the prophet's heart overflows; and in the third or last section the blessed condition of restored and converted Israel, who shall then be the channel and active propagators of the blessings of Messiah's gospel among all nations, is the outstanding subject.

The heart and climax of the whole prophecy is to be found in the brief section which forms its inmost centre (chaps. lii. 13 to liii. 12), which, instead of a prophecy uttered centuries in advance, reads like an historic summary of the Gospel narrative of the sufferings of the Christ and the glory that should follow.

Taking our position at this central point, we are almost overwhelmed with the evidence of design in the very structure of this prophecy, for on closer examination we find that each book is subdivided into three sections of three chapters each, nearly corresponding to the divisions in the Authorized Version. Thus the middle book is chapters xlix.–lvii. The middle section of the middle book is chapters lii., liii., liv., and chapter liii. is the middle chapter of the middle section of the middle book—forming, as it were, the heart and centre of this wonderful Messianic poem, as well as the heart and centre

of all Old Testament prophecy. The central verse of
this central paragraph, which begins properly with chap.
lii. 13, is : "*He was wounded for our transgressions, He
was bruised for our iniquities : the chastisement with a
view to our peace was upon Him ; and with His stripes
we are healed.*"

The doctrine it enshrines, namely, substitution, is one
of the leading truths unfolded in Old and New Testaments,
and it forms the central thought in this great prophecy.
It is, moreover, the essence of the message of comfort
with which the prophet begins (xl. 1, 2), solving the
problem as to how "her iniquity is pardoned."

CHAPTER II

THE ANCIENT JEWISH INTERPRETATION OF ISAIAH LIII.

THERE is truth in the observation of a scholarly writer that this great prophecy was "an enigma which could not be fully understood in the days before Christ, but which has been solved by the sufferings, death, resurrection, and exaltation of Him who was both Son of Man and Son of God."[1]

It is therefore not surprising to find that in the Talmud and Rabbinic Midrashim there is much confusion and contradiction in the various interpretations advanced by the Rabbis. But though it may be true, as Professor Dalman observes,[2] that the Messianic interpretation was not the general one, or the one officially recognized in Israel (any more than any of the other interpretations can be said to have been either generally or officially recognized), yet from most ancient times there have not been wanting authoritative teachers who interpreted the chapter of the Messiah—in spite of the fact that the picture of the Redeemer which is here drawn is utterly

---

[1] Dr. C. H. H. Wright, *The Servant of Jehovah.*
[2] Jesaja liii., *Das Prophetenwort. vom Sühnleiden des Heilmittlers.*

opposed to the disposition and to the perverted hopes and expectations in reference to the Messiah which have developed in Rabbinic Judaism.

In proof of this, the following few brief extracts from ancient Jewish interpretations will interest the Christian reader:

First, let me quote Jonathan ben Uzziel (first century A.D.), who begins his Targum with, "Behold, my Servant Messiah shall prosper; He shall be high and increase, and be exceeding strong." And then, to reconcile the interpretation of this scripture of the Messiah with his reluctance to recognize that the promised Deliverer must suffer and die for the sins of the nation, he proceeds to juggle with the scripture in a most extraordinary manner, making all the references to exaltation and glory n the chapter to apply to the Messiah, but the ireferences to tribulation and sufferings to Israel. In illustration of the method by which this is accomplished I need quote only his paraphrase of the very next verse (lii. 14), which reads: "As the House of Israel looked to Him during many days, because their countenance was darkened among the peoples, and their complexion beyond the sons of men."

In the Talmud Babylon,[1] among other opinions, we find the following: "The Messiah—what is His name? . . . The Rabbis say the 'leprous one';[2] (those) of the

---

[1] *Sanhedrin*, fol. 98*b*.

[2] This is based on a wrong interpretation of the word נָגוּעַ, *nagua'* —"stricken" or "plagued," as meaning "leprous."

house of Rabbi (say), 'the sick one,' as it is said, 'Surely He hath borne our sicknesses.'"[1]

That the generally received older Jewish interpretation of this prophecy was the Messianic is admitted by Abrabanel, who himself proceeds in a long polemic against the Nazarenes to interpret it of the Jewish nation. He begins: "The first question is to ascertain to whom (this scripture) refers: for the learned among the Nazarenes expound it of the man who was crucified in Jerusalem at the end of the second Temple, and who according to them was the Son of God and took flesh in the virgin's womb, as is stated in their writings. Jonathan ben Uzziel interprets it in the Targum of the future Messiah; and *this is also the opinion of our learned men in the majority of their Midrashim.*"

Similarly another (Rabbi Mosheh el Sheikh, commonly known as Alshech, second half of the sixteenth century), who also himself follows the older interpretation, at any rate of the first three verses (lii. 13–15, which, however, as we shall see when we come to the interpretation, contain a summary of the whole prophecy), testifies that *our*

---

[1] The other names of the Messiah mentioned in this passage are: "Shiloh,' with reference to Gen. xlix. 10, ''until Shiloh come''; "Yinnon," with reference to Ps. lxxii. 17, "His name shall endure for ever; before the sun (was created) his name was Yinnon"; "Haninah," in reference to Jer. xvi. 13, "where no Haninah (favour) will be given to you"; "M'nahem," son of Hezekiah, in reference to Lam. i. 16, ''the Comforter (M'nahem) that should restore my soul is far from me."

Rabbis with one voice accept and affirm the opinion that the prophet is speaking of the King Messiah.[1]

In fact, until Rashi[2] (Rabbi Solomon Yizchaki) applied it to the Jewish nation, the Messianic interpretation of this chapter was almost universally adopted by Jews, and his view, which we shall examine presently, although received by Aben Ezra, Kimchi, and others, was rejected as unsatisfactory by Maimonides, who is regarded by the Jews as of highest authority, by Alshech (as stated above), and many others, one of whom[3] says the interpretation adopted by Rashi "distorts the passage from its natural meaning," and that in truth "it was given of God as a description of the Messiah, whereby, when any should claim to be the Messiah, to judge by the resemblance or non-resemblance to it whether he were the Messiah or no." And another[4] says: "The meaning of 'He was wounded for our transgressions, . . . bruised for our iniquities,' is that since the Messiah bears our iniquities, which produce the effect of His being bruised, it follows that whoso will not admit that the Messiah thus suffers for our iniquities must endure and suffer for them himself."

---

[1] ‏הנה ר'ו'ל פה אחד קיימו וקבלו כי על מלך המשיח ידבר‎.

[2] Rashi, 1040–1105.

[3] R. Mosheh Kohen Iben Crispin, of Cordova, and afterwards of Toledo (fourteenth century). He rightly says of those who for controversial reasons applied this prophecy to Israel that by so doing "the doors of the literal interpretation of this Parashah were shut in their face, and that they wearied themselves to find the entrance, having forsaken the knowledge of our teachers, and inclined after the stubbornness of their own hearts and of their own opinions."

[4] R. Eliyya de Vidas, 1575 A.D.

Before proceeding to an examination of the modern Jewish interpretation of this chapter, let me add two further striking testimonies to its more ancient Messianic interpretation—taken this time, not from any Targum, or Midrash, or Rabbinical Commentary, which might be said to express the individual opinion of this or that Rabbi, but from the Jewish liturgy, which may be said to bear upon it the seal of the authority and usage of the whole Synagogue.

The first is taken from the Liturgy for the Day of Atonement—the most solemn day in the Jewish year—and reads as follows : " We are shrunk up in our misery even until now ! Our Rock hath not come nigh to us ; Messiah our righteousness (or ' our Righteous Messiah ') has departed from us : Horror hath seized upon us, and we have none to justify us.   He hath borne the yoke of our iniquities and our transgressions, and is wounded because of our transgression.   He beareth our sins on His shoulder, that He may find pardon for our iniquities. We shall be healed by His wound at the time the Eternal will create Him (Messiah) as a new creature.   O bring Him up from the circle of the earth, raise Him up from Seir to assemble us the second time on Mount Lebanon, by the hand of Yinnon." [1]

---

[1] This prayer or hymn forms part of the Musaph Service for the Day of Atonement. The author, according to Zunz (*Literatur geschichte der Syn. Poesie*, p. 56, etc.), was Eleazer ben Kalir, who lived in the ninth century. Yinnon, as will be seen from the quotation from Talmud Sanhedrin on p. 12, was one of the names given by the Rabbis to the Messiah, and is derived from Psalm lxxii. 17, which

The other passage is also from the *Machsor* (Liturgy for the Festival Services) and will be found among the prayers on the Feast of Passover. It is as follows: " Flee, my beloved, until the end of the vision shall speak; hasten, and the shadows shall take their flight hence : high and exalted and lofty shall be the despised one; he shall be prudent in judgment, and shall sprinkle many! Lay bare thine arm! cry out, and say: 'The voice of my beloved; behold he cometh!'"[1]

---

the Talmud renders, " Before the sun was, His name "—a rendering and explanation which implies a belief in the pre-existence of the Messiah.

[1] David Levi, the English translator of the *Machsor*, a Jew, says in a note that this verse referred to " the true Messiah."

CHAPTER III

THE MODERN JEWISH AND RATIONALISTIC CHRISTIAN INTERPRETATION OF ISAIAH LIII.

ON examining the different non-Messianic and controversial interpretations of this great prophecy, given by Jewish and unbelieving Christian Rabbis, it is an important fact to be borne in mind, as Pusey points out, that next to nothing turns upon renderings of the Hebrew. "The objections raised by Jewish controversialists (and I may add by the non-Messianic Christian interpreters) in only four, or at most five, words turn on the language." It is not then a question of knowledge of Hebrew Grammar, or Philology; and ordinary intelligent English readers, with the Authorized or Revised Version of the Scriptures in their hands, are well able to judge of the merits of the different interpretations which are advanced.

"The characteristics in which all agree are, that there would be a prevailing unbelief as to the subject of the prophecy, lowly beginnings, among circumstances outwardly unfavourable, but before God, and protected by Him; sorrows, injustice, contempt, death, which were the portion of the sufferer; that he was accounted a transgressor, yet that his sufferings were, in some way, vicarious, the just for the unjust; his meek silence; his willing acceptance of his death; his being with the rich in his death; his soul being (in some way) an offering for sin, and God's acceptance of it; his prolonged life; his making many righteous; his continued intercession for transgressors; the greatness of his exaltation, in proportion to the depth of his humiliation; the submission of kings to him; his abiding reign." [1]

Now these characteristics stand out in all literal translations (as distinguished from mere paraphrases) whether made by Jews or Christians, in the east or in the west. "The question," as the writer whom I have just quoted observes, "is not, 'What is the picture?'—in this all are agreed—but 'Whose image or likeness does it bear?'"

It is not necessary for us to examine those Jewish interpretations which apply this chapter to Jeremiah, Isaiah himself, Hezekiah, Josiah, or Job, etc., for they have been sufficiently refuted by Jewish writers themselves, but I may quote Hengstenberg's observation in reference to those Christian writers who have followed in the same lines.

"Among the interpretations which refer the prophecy to a single individual other than the Messiah," he says, "scarcely any one has found another defender than its own author. They are of importance only in so far as

---

[1] Pusey in his Introduction to *The Jewish Interpreters of Isaiah liii.*

2

they show that the prophecy does most decidedly make the impression that its subject is a real person, not a personification ; and further, that it could not by any means be an exegetical interest which induced rationalism to reject the interpretation which referred it to Christ."

The most generally accepted modern Jewish interpretation of this prophecy is that which makes it apply to the Jewish nation.

The first mention we have of this explanation is by Origen,[1] who, in his work against Celsus, says, " I remember once having used these prophecies in disquisition with those called wise among the Jews, whereon the Jews said that these things were prophesied of the whole people as one which was both dispersed abroad and smitten." But this may then have been the opinion of that particular Rabbi, or the counter-explanation may have been advanced by him (as has been done by later Rabbis and Jewish commentators) as a device, " in order to answer heretics " who were pressing them with the remarkable resemblance between the prophecy and its fulfilment in Jesus of Nazareth.

The first of the authoritative Jewish commentators who applied this chapter to the Jewish nation was Rashi, and since his time it has become more and more the "generally received" interpretation among the Jews. And that unbelieving Israel should have departed from the ancient interpretation which applied this prophecy to the Messiah is really not to be wondered at, for first

---

[1] Born, 185 or 186 A.D. ; died, 253.

the idea of a suffering expiatory Messiah became more and more repugnant to Rabbinic Judaism, which lost the knowledge of sin and the consciousness of the need of salvation, such as alone could make the doctrine of a vicariously suffering Redeemer acceptable. " Not knowing the holiness of God, and being ignorant of the true import of the Law," as Hengstenberg observes, "they imagine that in their own strength they can be justified before God. What they longed for was only an outward deliverance from their misery and oppressors, not an inward deliverance from sin. For this reason the Synagogue occupied itself exclusively with those Scriptures which announce a Messiah in glory, which passages also it misinterpreted."

Secondly, lacking or rejecting the key to the true understanding of this prophecy, namely, its fulfilment in Jesus of Nazareth, Jewish commentators were encountered by great difficulties and inexplicabilities in their attempts to expound it. This picture of a Messiah, which represented Him as passing through the deepest humiliation and suffering, and pouring out His soul unto death, appeared to them irreconcilable with those prophecies which speak of the Messiah as coming in power and glory.

And, thirdly, this explanation was not only " too flattering to the national feeling not to be extensively adopted,"[1] as Pusey observes, but it has really something

---

[1] " Every truly Christian reader feels humbled as he reads this portion of Scripture, because he sees in it a description of his

plausible from their point of view as its basis. Is not
Israel called *Ebhed Yehovah—the Servant of Jehovah*—in
this very Book of Isaiah? And has not Israel among
the nations suffered humiliations, and wrongs, and
tortures, and massacres, such as have been the lot or experience of no other people? In this connection it is an
interesting fact that the explanation of this chapter,
which made the Jewish nation to be the innocent sufferer
for the guilt of the other nations, originated in what has
been described as "the iron age of Judaism." Its
author, Rashi, at an earlier period of his life—when he
wrote his Commentary on the Talmud—actually followed
the older interpretation, which applied Isaiah liii. to the
Messiah, but he very probably wrote his Commentary
on the Bible (in which the new interpretation is first
introduced) after the second Crusade, when the hideous
massacres of Jews in Spire, Worms, Mainz, Cologne, by
the wild profligate swarm which gathered, after the first
Crusaders were gone, might well have occasioned it.
"Before the time of the first Crusade, the Jews in
Germany" (says the Jewish historian and apologist Graetz,

Saviour, and the cost of his redemption ; almost every Jew is likely
to feel lifted up, because he sees in it a description of the value of
Israel to the nations of the world, and of his own sufferings as a
means of peace and prosperity to Gentiles. There is thus a fundamental difference in the two interpretations of the chapter,
answering to the fundamental difference that there is between
Judaism and Christianity—the one a religion which magnifies human
efforts, the other one which makes humiliation of soul necessary to
true exaltation."—Canon A. Lukyn Williams in *Christian
Evidence for Jewish People.*

who counts as oppression any disparity of condition
between them and any people among whom they so-
journed) " were neither in a condition of oppression nor
contempt, nor were shut out from holding property. In
what has been called 'the iron age of Judaism,' there
was too much occasion for representing them (as far as
man was concerned) as guiltless sufferers."

To give Christian readers a good idea of what this
modern Jewish interpretation involves and how con-
sistently it is carried through, I reproduce the exposition
of Manasseh-ben-Israel,[1] which is an embodiment of
practically all that Jewish controversialists and rationalistic Christian writers who have followed on the same
lines, have to say on this subject. He calls his Commentary the *Reconciliation*, or an answer to the question,
" If this chapter is to be interpreted of the people of
Israel, how came Isaiah to say that it bore the sin of
many, whereas every one, according to the testimony
of Ezekiel, xviii. 20, pays only for his own guilt?" and
proceeds :

RECONCILIATION

" The subject of this question demands long argument,
and for our verses to be perfectly understood it will be
necessary to explain the whole of the chapter, which we
shall do with all possible brevity, without starting any
objections which may be made against other expositions,

---

[1] Born about 1604 ; died, 1657 ; Rabbi at Amsterdam ; advocate
before Cromwell and his Parliament for the readmission of Jews
into England.

as our intention is solely to show what our own opinion is. Accordingly, for greater clearness I shall set down the literal text with a paraphrase of my own, and then illustrate it by notes.

"Isaiah prophesies: (1) The extreme prosperity of Israel at the time of the Messiah. (2) The wonder of all the nations at seeing the rise from such a low state to grandeur. (3) How they will perceive their mistake, acknowledging themselves to be the sinners and Israel to be innocent. (4) What they will think of their various sects. (5) The patience of the people in suffering the troubles of the captivity; and the reward they will receive for their suffering.

Literal Translation.

Behold, my servant shall prosper; he shall be exalted, and shall be extolled, and shall be raised very high.

As many were astonished at thee, his visage was so marred more than any man, and his form more than the sons of man:

So will he cause many nations to speak; kings shall shut their mouths at him; what had not been told them they shall see; and what they had not heard they shall understand.

Paraphrase.

Behold, my servant Israel shall understand; he shall be exalted, extolled, and raised very high, at the coming of the Messiah.

As many of the nations were astonished at thee, O Israel, saying at the time of the captivity, Truly he is disfigured above all mankind in his countenance and form:

So at that time they shall speak of thy grandeur; even kings themselves shall shut their mouths in astonishment: for what they had never been told they shall see, and what they had not heard they shall understand.

Literal Translation.	*Paraphrase.*
Who will believe our report? and upon whom hath the arm of Adonai been manifested?	Who would have believed (the nations will say) what we see, had it been related to them? And look upon what a vile nation the arm of the Lord has manifested itself.
And he came up before him as a branch, and as a root out of a dry ground; he had no form nor comeliness; and we saw him, and there was no appearance that we should covet it.	He came up miraculously as a branch and a root out of a dry ground, for he had no form nor comeliness; we saw him, but so hideous, that it did not seem to us an appearance, for which we should envy him.
He was despised and rejected of men, a man of sorrows, accustomed to sickness; and as they hid their faces from him, he was despised, and we esteemed him not.	He was despised and rejected from the society of men, a man of sorrows, accustomed to suffer troubles; we hid our faces from him, he was despised and unesteemed among us.
Surely he bare our sicknesses, and endured our sufferings; and we esteemed him wounded, smitten by God, and afflicted.	But now we see that the sicknesses and troubles which we ought in reason to have suffered, he suffered and endured, and we thought that he was justly smitten by God and afflicted.
But he was pained by our transgressions, was crushed by our iniquities: the chastisement of our peace was upon him, and by his wounds we were healed.	Whereas he suffered the sicknesses and sufferings which we deserved for our sins: he bore the chastisement which our peace and felicity deserved; but his troubles appear to have been the cure of ourselves.
All we like sheep went astray, we turned every one to his own way; and Adonai (God) caused the sin of all to meet upon him.	All we like sheep went astray: we followed every one his own sect, and so the Lord seems to have transferred on him the punishment of us all.

Literal Translation.

Paraphrase.

He was oppressed, and he was afflicted, and he opened not his mouth ; he was carried as a lamb to the slaughter and was dumb as a sheep before its shearers ; and he opened not his mouth.

He was taken from imprisonment and judgment, and who shall declare his generation? for he was cut off from the land of the living : for the transgression of my people they were stricken.

And he made his grave with the wicked, and with the rich in his deaths, although he had not acted falsely and there was no deceit in his mouth.

And Adonai wished to crush him, made him sick : if he offer his soul as an expiation, he shall see seed, he shall prolong days, and the will of Adonai shall prosper in his hand.

From the trouble of his soul he shall see, shall be satisfied : by his wisdom my righteous servant shall justify many : and he shall bear their iniquities.

Therefore I will distribute to him with many, and with the

He was oppressed and afflicted : he was taken by us as a lamb to the slaughter and as a sheep before its shearers, depriving him of life and property : and he was dumb and opened not his mouth.

From prison and these torments he is now delivered : and who would have thought of this his happy age when he was banished from the holy land? Through the wickedness of my people (each nation will say) this blow came upon them.

He was buried with malefactors, and suffered various torments with the rich, without having committed crime or used deceit with his mouth.

But it was the Lord (the prophet says) who wished to make him sick and afflict him, in order to purify him : if he offer his soul as an expiation, he shall see seed, he shall prolong his days, and the will and determination of the Lord shall prosper in his hand.

For the trouble which his soul suffered in captivity, he shall see good, shall be satisfied with days : by his wisdom my righteous servant Israel shall justify the many, and he will bear their burdens.

Therefore I will give him his share of spoil among the many

Literal Translation.   *Paraphrase.*

strong he shall divide the spoil: because he gave up his soul unto death, and was numbered with the transgressors, and he bare the sin of many: and he prayed for the transgressors.

and powerful of Gog and Magog, because he gave himself up unto death for the sanctification of my name; and was numbered with the transgressors; and he bare the offence of many, even praying for the very transgressors from whom he received injuries."

Of his "Commentary" I am only able, for lack of space, to reproduce his notes on those verses which speak particularly of the vicariousness of the sufferings of Jehovah's righteous servant. He says, on chap. lii. 13 :

"'Servant' was one of the many titles of honour with which the blessed God honoured Israel (Isa. xli. 8; Jer. xxx. 10; Ezek. xxxvii. 25; Ps. cxxxvi. 22). And as the prophet in this chapter praises the fidelity with which Israel, as loyal servants, were ever in the service of the blessed Lord, suffering innumerable persecutions in this captivity, he therefore applies this title to them here. Whence it appears that the sole subject of this prophecy is the people of Israel; and that is the true meaning of it; and the certainty of this is further proved by its connection with the preceding chapter, where the prophet says, 'Awake, awake; put on thy strength, O Zion,' etc. (lii. 1–12); and then he continues (ver. 13), 'Behold my servant shall prosper, or understand, etc.'

"The prophet addresses himself to the people, and shows that in the same manner as the nations of the

world wondered at their low estate and fortunes, even
going so far as to charge them with being disfigured,
having a form unsuitable to man, and unlike other
mortals, so at that period will they wonder at their
prosperity and elevated state; for, seeing the sudden
change in the fortune of Israel, rising from such extreme
meanness to such extensive empire, all the kings of the
earth will wonder and discourse on the subject. And he
gives the reason of this, namely, because what had never
been told them of any nation they see in the people of
Israel, whose grandeur none ever equalled, and what
they had never heard from their false teachers, they now
understand. Or יִקְפְּצוּ, *yiqp'tsu*, signifies *they will shut
their mouth*, speaking with great respect and modesty
of that people which they had shortly before known as
captives, subject to the will of their tyrannous power
(Mic. vii. 15–16)."

On verses 4–7 he puts the following words into the
mouth of the Gentile nations: "We unbelievers more
justly merited the troubles and calamities which this
innocent people suffered in their captivity. But we were
so blind that we considered him to be wounded, smitten,
and afflicted by God, and not through ourselves, and that
all this came on them for keeping themselves apart from
the truth, and not joining with us in our religion.

"But it was quite the contrary, for our wickedness
alone was the cause of his troubles; did they not arise
from any hatred God bore them. *The punishment*
(מוּסָר, *musar*) *or discipline of our peace*, was upon him, for,

as grief always accompanies pleasure, the chastisement
of this happiness appears to have fallen on him. Or
it may also mean, when in the enjoyment of peace
adversaries were wanting, we immediately turned our
arms against this people, and what we established for
the discipline and good government of our states all
redounded in measures against him, decrees of death,
banishment, and confiscation of property, as experience
daily shows. Or otherwise, the doctrine (מוּסָר, *musar*)
taught by our preachers was that our tranquillity de
pended upon our being irritated against him, and
ultimately we should find health in wounding him.

" *But all we like sheep went astray, etc.* That is, they
will not only acknowledge the ill-treatment and bodily
inflictions they had made Israel suffer, but at the same
time their errors, attributing their wickedness thereto ;
for many will say, We all (Ishmaelites and Idumeans)
like sheep went astray, each in his own way following a
new sect, just as the prophet Jeremiah says (xvi. 19).
And the Lord made to fall on him the wickedness of us
all. That is, we erred ; they followed the truth ; consequently they suffered the punishments which we
deserved.

" We deprived them of their property as tribute, and
afflicted their bodies with various kinds of torture, yet
he opened not his mouth, etc. The experience of this
is seen every day, particularly in the cruelties of the
Inquisition, and the false testimony raised against them
to take their wool and rob them of their property. And

it is exactly this that the Psalmist says, 'Thou hast given us, O Lord, like sheep appointed for meat' (xliv. 12); and further on, 'For thy sake are we killed every day; we are counted as sheep for the slaughter' (xliv. 23), suffering daily with the greatest patience these acts of tyranny and fearful calamities."

On verse 9 he says: "The nations continue, We have frequently condemned this people to death, and buried them with malefactors, and with the rich, בְּמוֹתָיו, in their various deaths, though it is certain that, in order to take away their property, we raised against them innumerable false testimonies, and martyred them, without them having committed any crime or our having any charge against them, except of having accumulated wealth, as he continues, although he had committed no חָמָס, robbery, and there was no deceit in his mouth, that is, allowing themselves to be robbed of the property they had not robbed, and to be killed for the sanctification of the Lord, and refusing to acknowledge with their mouth any other religion.

"From verse 10 onward the prophet speaks in the name of the Lord, and relates the reason why these troubles were suffered, and the reward to be hoped from them. And, firstly, he says that the will and determination of the Lord has been to crush them and to make them sick by so many different calamities, that, being purified by these means, they may become worthy of such great felicity. *If he offer his soul as an expiation*, אָשָׁם, surrendering it for the sake of the Law; or, if he give himself up and acknowledge himself guilty, becoming repentant, as Joseph's brethren, who said, 'But we are guilty' (Gen. xlii. 21), *he shall see seed*, that is, they shall multiply infinitely (Ezek. xxxvi. 37; Zech. x. 10; Deut. xxx. 5). *He shall prolong days.* The same prophet confirms this where he says, 'As the days of the tree,' that is, the tree of life, 'are the days of my people' (lxv. 22); and Zechariah, 'And every man with his staff in his hand from multitude of days' (viii. 4). Lastly, and *the will of the Lord*, which is to oppress him and make him sick with punishments for his greater glory, *shall prosper in his hand*, for the purpose and end to which they are directed will be attained. Or, the will of the Lord, which is that all should be saved and come to the holy knowledge of himself, will prosper through his hand and means and take effect.

"*By his knowledge my righteous servant shall justify many.* That is, Israel, who is termed 'a righteous people and holy nation,' justifies many by his knowledge and wisdom, bringing them with brotherly love over to the true religion, and separating them from their vain sects; and this at the very time that he bears their iniquities, patiently suffering the tyranny of their wickedness. Or it may otherwise mean, At that time my servant Israel will justify and make many nations meritorious (Mic. iv. 2; Zech. viii. 23).

"*And he shall bear their iniquities.* For, being a most religious and holy people, he will take charge of the spiritual administration of the observance of the Law as Moses says to Aaron, 'Thou and thy sons with thee shall bear the iniquity of the sanctuary' (Num. xviii. 1).

"*Because he poured out his soul unto death, etc.* The prophet here attributes four merits to them, for which they justly deserve the reward of that happiness; and again in the form of a compendium he recapitulates the contents of the chapter. (1) Because he delivered himself up to death, allowing himself to be killed for the sanctification of the Lord's name and the observance of His most holy Law. (2) Because he was reckoned among the wicked, patiently enduring to be called a heretic. (3) For having borne the sin of many, the wickedness and tyranny of others falling on his shoulders. (4) Lastly, in having observed the precept of Jeremiah, 'Seek the welfare of the city whither I have caused you to be carried captive' (xxix. 7); and this, too, so carefully that in all their prayers they pray for the health of the prince, and the peace of the kingdom or province wherein they reside; and, what is more, it may be even for the welfare of those from whom they are receiving insult and wrong, which is highly meritorious, and a convincing proof of the constancy and patience with which they receive from the Lord's hand the yoke of captivity and the sufferings of its misfortunes."

This, then, is the modern Jewish view of this prophecy. "Among Christians," to quote the words of a great German Bible student, "the interpretation has taken nearly the same course as among the Jews

Similar causes have produced similar effects in both cases. By both, the true explanation was relinquished, when the prevailing tendencies had become opposed to its results. And if we descend to particulars, we shall find a great resemblance even between the modes of interpretation proposed by both. Even *a priori*, we could not but suppose otherwise than that the Christian Church, as long as she possessed Christ, found Him here also, where He is so clearly and distinctly set before our eyes—that as long as she in general still acknowledged the authority of Christ and of the Apostles, she could not but, here too, follow their distinct, often-repeated testimony. And so, indeed, do we find it to be. With the exception of a certain Silesian called Seidel—who, given up to total unbelief, asserted that the Messiah had never yet come, nor would ever come—and of Grotius, both of whom supposed Jeremiah to be the subject—no one of the Christian Church has, for seventeen centuries, ventured to call in question the Messianic interpretation.

" On the contrary, this passage was always considered to be the most distinct and glorious of all the Messianic prophecies. It was reserved to the last quarter of the eighteenth century to be the first to reject the Messianic interpretation. *At a time when Naturalism exercised its sway, it could no longer be retained.* For, if this passage contains a Messianic prophecy at all, its contents offer so striking an argument with the history of Christ that its origin cannot at all be accounted for in the natural way. Expedients were therefore sought for ; and these were so much the more easily found that the Jews had, in this matter, already opened up the way.

"All that was necessary was only to appropriate their arguments and counter-arguments, and to invest them with the semblance of solidity by means of a learned apparatus."

CHAPTER IV

THE UNTENABLENESS OF THE MODERN INTERPRETATION

I shall now proceed to show the untenableness of this modern interpretation; but before doing so it is necessary to point out that, like most of the false teaching of the present day, it contains a germ of truth which lends plausibility to the error.

The germ of truth contained in this explanation is that, as has already been observed above, the term "Servant of Jehovah" is indeed again and again applied to Israel in the second half of the Book of Isaiah. Thus, in the very first instance where the phrase occurs, we read: "*But thou, Israel, art My servant, Jacob whom I have chosen, the seed of Abraham My friend.*"[1] Again: "*Ye are My witnesses, saith Jehovah, and My servant whom I have chosen: that ye may know and believe Me, and understand that I am He.*"[2]

"*Yet now hear, O Jacob My servant; and Israel, whom I have chosen,*" etc.[3]

This is Israel's high calling, but, alas! in this, as in

---

[1] Isa. xli. 8.   [2] Isa. xliii. 10.   [3] Isa. xliv. 1.

the other great relationships to God, to which he was called, namely, that of a son to his father, and of a wife to her husband, Israel has failed and proved himself unfaithful.

Israel's failure to apprehend that for which he was apprehended of God, and his unfaithfulness as Jehovah's *Servant*, is forcibly depicted in many passages in these very chapters of Isaiah. "*Hear, ye deaf*," God complains in the 42nd chapter; "*and look, ye blind, that ye may see. Who is blind, but My servant? or deaf, as My messenger that I send? Who is blind as he that was called to be perfect* (or '*as he that is at peace*'), *and blind as Jehovah's servant? Seeing many things, but thou observest not; his ears are open, but he heareth not.*"[1]

But Israel's sins and disobedience cannot frustrate the purpose of God. The ideal to which the nation could not rise is gloriously realized in Him who is both the Head and Heart of Israel. In the words of Von Orelli, "The idea, Servant of Jehovah, which was united from the first in God's purpose with the people of Israel, outgrew this national limit, even as the idea, 'Son of God,' which was likewise at first attributed to the people, also became a separate Person and was definitely assigned to the Messiah — *i.e.* the Lord's Anointed" (as, for instance, in Ps. ii.). It is true that both these designations ("Servant" and "Son") remain as marks of the *character indelebilis* impressed by God's grace on this nation, and in and through their Messiah, and in

---

[1] Isa. xlii. 18–20.

union with Him, will yet become true of their actual
condition and experience; hence, wherever this *grace*
speaks, and restored and converted Israel in the future
is prophetically contemplated, the nation still wears these
names of honour, as, for instance, in the passages
from chapters xli., xliii., and xliv., quoted above. "But
the more the nation as a whole shows itself incapable of
rising to the high calling implied in it, and the less the
Lord is willing to renounce the realizing of this high
idea, the more plainly the term 'Servant of Jehovah'
detaches itself from the national multitude and becomes
a personally conceived ideal, which acquires such inde-
pendence that the nation itself becomes the object of
the Servant's redeeming work." [1] In chapter xlix. especially we see this One Individual who is out of the nation,

[1] The following suggestive note is from Franz Delitzsch on
Isaiah : "The idea of the Servant of Jehovah assumed, so to
speak, figuratively, the form of a pyramid. The base was Israel as
a whole ; the central section was that Israel which was not merely
Israel according to the flesh, but according to the spirit also ; the
apex is the person of the Mediator of Salvation springing out of
Israel. And the last of the three is regarded (1) as the centre of the
circle of the promised kingdom—the second David ; (2) the centre
of the circle of the people of salvation—the second Israel ; (3) the
centre of the human race—the second Adam. Throughout the
whole of these prophecies, in chapters xl.–lxvi., the knowledge of
salvation is still in its second stage, and about to pass into the third.
Israel's true nature as a servant of God, which had its roots in the
election and calling of Jehovah, and manifested itself in conduct
and action in harmony with its calling, is all concentrated in Him
the One, as its ripest fruit. The gracious purposes of God toward
the whole human race, which were manifested even in the election
of Israel, are brought by Him to their full completion.

and yet towering high above it, invested with the name and the mission to which the whole people was called in the first instance.

"*Listen, O isles, unto me; and hearken, ye peoples, from far; Jehovah hath called me from the womb; from the bowels of my mother hath He made mention of my name.*

"*And He hath made my mouth like a sharp sword; in the shadow of His hand hath He hid me, and He hath made me a polished shaft; in His quiver hath He kept me close;*

"*And He said unto me, Thou art My servant, Israel, in whom I will be glorified.*

"*But I said, I have laboured in vain, I have spent my strength for nought, and for vanity: yet surely my judgment is with Jehovah, and my recompence with my God.*

"*And now, saith Jehovah that formed me from the womb to be His servant, to bring Jacob again to Him, and that Israel be gathered unto Him: (for I am honourable in the eyes of Jehovah, and my God is become my strength :)*

"*Yea, He saith, It is too light a thing that thou shouldest be My servant to raise up the tribes of Jacob, and to restore the preserved of Israel: I will give thee for a light to the Gentiles, and that thou mayest be My salvation unto the end of the earth.*"[1]

That it is not of the nation of Israel that this prophecy speaks is clear, and manifest to every unbiased mind,

---

[1] Isa. xlix. 1-6.

since the One who is here thus dramatically introduced as proclaiming His own call and enduement for His office, and whom Jehovah addresses, is the One who is sent as *the Redeemer of Israel*, namely, "to raise up the tribes of Jacob and to restore the preserved of Israel," *i.e.* not only to their land, but to *their God.*

Here God says to him, "Thou art My servant, O Israel" (or, "Thou art Israel"). He is invested with the name of Israel because He, "as Israel's inmost centre, as Israel's highest head," realizes the idea and carries out the mission to which the nation which had originally been *called* to the task of carrying out God's saving purpose in relation to the world does not respond.

Here, too, as in chapter xlii. 1–9, where the ideal personal Servant of Jehovah is contrasted with the nation whose failure and unfaithfulness is depicted in verses 18–25 of the same chapter, His mission extends, not only to Israel, whom He is to raise up and restore, and to whom He is to be, not only the mediator, but the very embodiment of "the covenant" which shall be everlastingly established between them and their God, but is to be the light also of the Gentiles, and God's salvation unto the very ends of the earth.

And as in chapters xlii. and xlix., so also in Isa. liii. itself, "where the figure of the Servant of Jehovah unfolds its entire fullness of meaning," He is clearly and definitely distinguished from the nation. Thus, for instance, we read in the 8th verse, "*For the transgressions*

of my people was He stricken." The speaker is either
Jehovah or the prophet, but in either case עַמִּי, *ami,*
"my people," can apply only to Israel, and if the servant
is stricken for Israel he cannot be Israel.   But, apart
from the fact that in chapters xlii. 1–9, xlix. 1–7, l. 4–11,
liii. (which begins lii. 13), and lxi., this ideal Servant
stands out clearly distinguished from the nation, there
are other conclusive reasons why the 53rd chapter in
particular cannot be applied to Israel, for (1) the subject
of the prophecy is an absolutely innocent sufferer who
suffers for the guilt of others—one who has Himself "done
no violence, nor can deceit be found in His mouth," but
is "stricken," "smitten," and "afflicted of God" for
others.   (2) He is a *voluntary* sufferer—one who willingly "pours out His own soul unto death" (ver. 12).
(3) He is an *unresisting* sufferer—one who is "led
as a lamb to the slaughter and as a sheep before her
shearers is dumb, He openeth not His mouth"; and
(4) His sufferings end *in death.*

Now, none of these points is found in the Jewish
nation.   Israel has been suffering, and is suffering as no
other nation has suffered.   Truly "under the whole
heaven," to use the words of Daniel, "hath not been
done as hath been done upon Jerusalem" and upon her
people during the many centuries of their dispersion.   I
have elsewhere given a condensed summary of the
terrible story of Israel's sufferings since the destruction
of the second Temple,[1] and of the guilt incurred by the

---

[1] See *The Shepherd of Israel and His Scattered Flock.*

nations by their cruel conduct towards them, but Israel is not an innocent sufferer. Israel's sorrows and sufferings are the direct consequence of his sins.

Modern Rabbis, in spite of the definite statement in the chapter itself, that it was "for the transgressions of My people" (Israel) that the righteous servant was stricken, put verses 1–9 into the mouth of the Gentile nations, and make *them* say that "he (*i.e.* Israel) suffered the sickness and sufferings which we Gentiles deserved"; but this is only part of the self-deception which characterizes the modern teachers and leaders of the Synagogue, and which has led them to perversive views of their own Scriptures and facts of history. It is this same spirit of pharisaic self-satisfaction which regards the dispersion among the nations as a blessing, and denies the necessity of atonement and of a mediator between God and man.

But whether we will heed or not, the solemn fact remains that Israel's dispersion among the nations, and their many sufferings during the long period of their wanderings from the presence of God, are the direct consequences of their apostasy and sin.

At the very beginning of their history Moses foretold what the consequences would be if they departed from their God. "*If ye will not for all this hearken unto Me, but walk contrary unto Me, then I will walk contrary unto you in fury: and I also will chastise you seven times for your sins. . . . And I will make your cities a waste and your sanctuaries a desolation. . . . And you will I scatter among the nations, and I will draw out the sword after*

*you. . . . And you shall perish among the nations, and
the land of your enemies shall eat you up.   And they that
are left of you* (far from atoning by their sufferings for
the sins of the Gentile nations) *shall pine away in their
iniquity in your enemies' lands.   And also in the iniquities
of their fathers shall they pine away with them.*"   And
this is to last until "*they shall confess their iniquities, and
the iniquity of their fathers in their trespass which they
trespassed against Me, and also that because they walked
contrary unto Me. . . .   If then their uncircumcised heart
be humbled and they accept of the punishment of their
iniquity, then will I remember My covenant with Jacob ;
and also My covenant with Isaac, and also My covenant
with Abraham will I remember ; and I will remember the
land.*"[1]

And what Moses announced in advance in Lev. xxvi.
and Deut. xxviii., etc., is repeated and confirmed by all
the prophets.   We need only contemplate the picture of
Israel as a nation given in this Book of Isaiah itself to be
convinced that it cannot be of it that the prophet speaks
in chapter liii.   Far from being itself absolutely innocent
(as the Servant of Jehovah in Isa. liii. is described as
being) and suffering for the guilt of others, the prophet
speaks of them as "*a sinful nation, a people laden with
iniquity, a seed of evildoers,*"[2] whose iniquities have
separated between them and their God, and whose sins
have caused His face to be hid from them that He will
not hear.[3]

---

[1] Lev. xxvi. 14-45.   [2] Isa. i. 2-9.   [3] Isa. lix. 2-15.

In the 42nd chapter Israel's suffering condition among the nations is described in graphic style and language. "*But this is a people robbed and plundered; they are all of them snared in holes, and they are hid in prison houses: they are for a prey, and none delivereth; for a spoil, and none saith, Restore.*" But the prophet proceeds immediately to declare that Israel's sorrows and sufferings are not the result of mere chance, but are due to the direct acts of God in judgment on account of Israel's sins. "*Who is there among you that will give ear to this, that will hearken and hear for the time to come? Who gave Jacob for a spoil, and Israel to the robbers? Did not Jehovah? He against whom we have sinned, and in whose ways they would not walk, neither were they obedient unto His law.*" [1]

To evade the force of this truth, that the nation could not be the innocent sufferer set forth in the personal portraiture of the Servant of Jehovah in chapters xlii., xlix., l., liii., and lxi., some Jewish and rationalistic writers have interpreted this great prophecy of the godly remnant in the nation. But, though relatively the pious in the nation may be spoken of as righteous when compared with the godless majority, they are not absolutely righteous, and, far from being able to render a vicarious satisfaction for others, they cannot even stand themselves before God on the ground of their own righteousness.

It is indeed the godly remnant in the nation which is described in the second part of Isaiah as of "a contrite

---

[1] Isa. xlii. 23–25.

and humble spirit," who are themselves waiting for the salvation of God, which will be wholly of *grace*. It is *they*—"the righteous ones"—who confess for themselves and the entire nation that "we are *all* become as one that is unclean, *and all our righteousnesses are as a polluted garment; and we all do fade as a leaf; and our iniquities, like the wind, take us away.*" [1]

It is perfectly true, therefore, that Isaiah speaks of the "*entire* nation as needing enlightening, redeeming, and reconciling to God," and the godly remnant of it, far from being represented in these chapters as rendering satisfaction for others by their sufferings, "appears on the contrary a fainting flock which the Servant of Jehovah is to release, and refresh, and for whose justification He is to suffer and die." [2]

And as Israel is not an innocent sufferer so neither does he suffer *voluntarily*. "The Jews did not go voluntarily into captivity," as Hengstenberg well observes, "but were dragged into it by force," and so all through the centuries they did not voluntarily suffer the many oppressions and wrongs which they had to endure, but were forced to submit to them by the Gentile nations whom God used as His scourge.

Still less can it be asserted that Israel was an *unresisting* sufferer. "Here is one described," writes another Hebrew Christian brother, "who bears all sorts of affliction and oppression, without making the slightest resistance, without even opening his mouth to utter reproach

---

[1] Isa. lxiv. 6.   [2] Von Orelli.

—one who has the meekness and gentleness of a lamb, the inoffensiveness of a sheep. Surely this does not apply to the Jews. A very hasty glance at their history is sufficient to convince us of that. As long as ever they had the power, they did resist bitterly and bloodily. We freely acknowledge that their provocations were great. We have no wish to defend the wickedness of Christian nations. We grant that their treatment of the Jews is a blot and a stain. But that is not the question. The question is, Did the Jews bear all the oppression heaped upon them like lambs? Did they suffer evil without resisting it? History answers in the negative. The history of the Jewish captivity for the first seven centuries is a history of a series of insurrections, fierce and violent, against the nations. How desperate was the resistance to the Roman power which brought on the destruction of the temple by Titus! But when that was destroyed, the spirit of resistance still remained. A.D. 115, the Jews of Cyrene rebelled and slew 220,000 Libyans; and it was not until after several bloody battles that they submitted. A.D. 132, Bar Cochba appeared in the character of the Messiah at the head of an army, ready to shake off the Roman yoke. R. Akiba, one of those looked upon by the Rabbis as most right-eous, supported his resistance to the Roman authority; a bloody war was the consequence, and it was only by force that this insurrection was put down. A.D. 415, the Jews of Alexandria revolted. A.D. 522, the Jews of Persia revolted under the conduct of R. Mid, or Miz, at

their head, and declared war against the King of Persia.
A.D. 535, the Jews in Cæsarea rebelled. A.D. 602, the
Jews at Antioch. A.D. 624, the Jews in Arabia took up
arms against Mahomet. A.D. 613, they joined the
armies of Chosroes, when he made himself master of
Jerusalem, and put thousands to death." [1]

Neither have the sufferings of the Jewish nation ended
in death, as is the lot of the Servant of Jehovah in Isa.
liii. No; Israel, in spite of all the centuries of persecutions and oppressions, still lives and can say as of yore,
"Many a time have they afflicted me from my youth, yet
they have not prevailed against me." "I shall not die,
but live, and declare the works of Jehovah."

I must bring this introductory section to a close, but

---

[1] *Doctrine and Interpretation of the Fifty-Third Chapter of Isaiah*,
by Dr. Alexander M'Caul.

And yet in spite of these facts a modern Jewish writer (Dr. A.
Kohut, in *Discussions on Isaiah lii. 13–liii. 12*) can allow himself
to write : "We have suffered much and murmured less ; the
annals of history teem with the atrocious crimes of cruel Torque-
madas, but fail to reproach us with even a breath of remonstrance.
. . . We have whispered sweetly of our wrongs, not imprecations of
revenge, but hope-fraught hymns of glad release." But it is a fact, as
Dr. Lukyn Williams observes in reply, that "meekness is not, and
never has been, a characteristic of Jews, and they have not hesitated
to call down the vengeance of God upon their enemies in their private
or public devotions. So, for example, in the Service for the Festival
of the Dedication : 'When Thou shalt have prepared a slaughter of
the blaspheming foe, I will complete with song and psalm the dedication of Thy altar,' and, at the end of the same piece, though
omitted by Dr. Singer : 'Lay bare Thy holy arm, and bring the
time of Thy salvation near. Take vengeance for the blood of Thy
servants from the wicked nation'" (*Christian Evidence for Jewish
People*, by Canon A. Lukyn Williams, vol. i. p. 168).

I may add to all that has been said that it is clear and
manifest to all unprejudiced minds that the chapter
cannot be applied to a collective body personified, but
must refer to an individual person. To quote from
another writer, "Not one analogous instance can be
quoted in favour of a personification carried on through a
whole section, without the slightest intimation that it is
not a single individual who is spoken of. In verse 3 the
subject is called אִישׁ (*ish*, 'a man'); in verses 10 and 12
a soul is ascribed to Him; grave and death are used so
as to imply a subject in the singular. Scripture never
leaves anything to be guessed. If we had an allegory
before us, distinct hints as to the interpretation would
certainly not be wanting. It is, *e.g.*, quite different in
those passages where the prophet designates Israel by
the name of the Servant of the Lord. In them, all
uncertainty is prevented by the addition of the names of
'Jacob' and 'Israel';[1] and in them, moreover, the prophet uses the plural by the side of the singular to
intimate that the Servant of the Lord is an ideal person,
a collective."[2]

No, this prophecy speaks of an individual, and there
is only one person in the history of the world whom it
fits. "Let any one steep his mind in the contents of
this chapter," observes Professor James Orr, "and then
read what is said about Jesus in the Gospels, and as
he stands under the shadow of the Cross, say if there is

---

[1] Compare Isa. xli. 8, xliv. 1, 2, 21, xlv. 4, xlviii. 20.
[2] *E.g.* xliii. 10–14, xlviii. 20, 21.

not the most perfect correspondence between the two.
In Jesus of Nazareth alone in all history, but in Him
perfectly, has this prophecy found fulfilment. The
meekness, the pathos of undeserved suffering, the atoning
function, the final triumph, will suit no other." That
there is a marked resemblance between the picture of
the Servant of Jehovah in this chapter and the historic
account of Jesus of Nazareth as given in the Gospels is
acknowledged by many Jews.

Thus Rabbi Abraham Farissol,[1] who himself proceeds
to misinterpret the prophecy of Israel, says : " In this
chapter there seem to be considerable resemblances
and allusions to the work of the Christian Messiah and
to the events which are asserted to have happened to
him—so that no other prophecy can be found, the gist
and subject of which can be so immediately applied to
him." And as a matter of fact this glorious prophecy of
the sufferings of the Messiah and the glory which should
follow has been used of God more than any Scripture
in opening the eyes of Jews to recognize in Jesus Israel's
Redeemer-King.[2]

---

[1] Rabbi Farissol, early in the sixteenth century, author of *Iggereth
Orechoth Olam ; Itinera Mundi.*

[2] " Blessed, precious chapter, how many of God's ancient covenant people have been led by thee to the foot of Christ's cross !—
that cross over which was written, ' Jesus Christ, the King of the
Jews !' And oh ! what a glorious commentary shall be given of
thee when, in the latter days, repentant and believing Israel,
looking unto Him whom they have pierced, shall exclaim, ' Surely
He hath borne our griefs, and carried our sorrows ; yet we did

Is this, perhaps, the chief reason why this chapter is omitted from the public readings in the Synagogue? We know, of course, that whereas the whole *Torah* (the Pentateuch) is read through on the Sabbaths in the course of the year, only selections from the prophets are appointed for the *Haphtarahs*, but it is none the less remarkable that in these "selections" the portion for one Sabbath should end with the 12th verse of the 52nd chapter, and the one for the following should begin with the 54th chapter, and that the whole of this sublime section about the suffering Servant, through the knowledge of whom the many are made righteous, is passed over.

It certainly gives ground for the statement that the 53rd of Isaiah is "the bad conscience of the Synagogue," which it dare not face because it reminds them too much of Him whom the nation, alas! in its blindness still despises and rejects, and considers "smitten of God and afflicted." But this very feeling and attitude on the part of the Jewish nation is one great proof that Jesus is the Messiah, and that it is to Him that this prophecy refers.

---

esteem Him stricken, smitten of God, and afflicted!'"—Adolph Saphir, D.D., *The Sinner and the Saviour.*

PART II

THE EXPOSITION

"Then Philip opened his mouth, and began at the same
scripture, and preached unto him Jesus."—ACTS viii. 35.

CHAPTER I

JEHOVAH'S INTRODUCTION OF HIS SERVANT AND
A SUMMARY OF HIS REDEEMING WORK

THE DIVISIONS

WE will now seek, apart from controversy and criticisms, to look into the heart of this great prophecy, and I will make no further apologies if in the handling of this chapter I do so in the full light which is thrown upon it in the New Testament as well as the Old. The whole prophecy divides itself into three sections.

The first section consists of verses 13–15 of chapter lii., and may be described as God's *Ecce Homo*. In it God introduces His Servant, and seeks to direct the attention of all men to Him. This introductory section is really a summary of the whole prophecy, and contains in brief the whole story of Messiah's sufferings and the glory which should follow.

The second section, consisting of verses 1–9 of chapter liii., is primarily the lament and confession of penitent Israel in the future, when the spirit of grace and of supplications shall be poured upon them, and their eyes are opened to behold Him whom they have pierced.

The third section, consisting of the last three verses, sets forth the blessed fruit of Messiah's sufferings, or the glory which should follow.

The prophecy really begins and ends with a description of the exaltation and glory of the Righteous Servant, but in between the mountain-tops of glory lies the deep valley of shame and suffering, which "for us men and our salvation" He has to pass.

"Behold My Servant"

The prophecy begins with the word הִנֵּה, *hinneh* ("behold").

This is the little word by which in Scripture God seeks to call the attention of men to matters which are of the utmost importance for them to know. Here it is on His beloved and only-begotten Son in the form of a servant that He would have our eyes fixed.

We may note in passing that several different times is the Messiah introduced in the Old Testament by this word "behold," and in four different aspects. Here (as in Zech. iii. 8, which refers back to the passages about the Servant of Jehovah in the second part of Isaiah) it is "Behold *My Servant.*"

In Zech. vi. 12 we read, "Behold *the Man* whose name is the Branch"; and in chap. ix. 9 of the same prophecy, the announcement to the daughter of Zion is, "Behold, *thy King* cometh unto thee"; while the proclamation in the sublime prologue to the second half of Isaiah unto the cities of Judah is, "*Behold your God*";

and that it is of the Epiphany of God in the person of the Messiah that the prophet speaks is evident from the whole context of those chapters. Under these four different aspects also is Messiah spoken of by the name of "Branch"—"the Branch of Jehovah" (Isa. iv. 2); "the Branch of David" (Jer. xxiii. 5, 6); "My Servant, the Branch" (Zech. iii. 8); and "the Man whose name is the 'Branch'" (Zech. vi. 12).

The Man—the Servant—the Son of David—and the Son of God.

And this fourfold portraiture of the Redeemer in the Old Testament corresponds (as I first pointed out in a small work many years ago)[1] to the fourfold picture of our Saviour in the New Testament.

We have four different and independent accounts of the Life of Christ, and so harmonious and similar are the main features and facts about His character and work in all the Four Gospels that no one who has ever read them has had to be told that they all speak of the same blessed Person. Yet each one of the Evangelists was led by the Spirit of God to portray a different aspect of His character.

Over the Gospel of Matthew—which was primarily written for the Jews, and which sets forth Christ as the Redeemer-King of Israel, the Messiah promised to the fathers—the inscription may be written, "Behold thy *King*."

---

[1] *Rays of Messiah's Glory*, now out of print. The subject is also more fully dealt with in the exposition of the 3rd chapter of Zechariah in *The Visions and Prophecies of Zechariah*.

Over the Gospel of Mark—a summary more of His deeds than of His words, written, in the first instance, for the practical Roman world of power and action—the words, "Behold My *Servant*," are, so to say, inscribed, for there it is the *Servant* aspect of our Saviour that is portrayed before us—"how God anointed Him with the Holy Spirit and with power; who went about doing good, and healing all that were oppressed with the devil; for God was with Him."

In the Gospel of Luke, written primarily for the Greek, who, in the New Testament, stands as the representative of the Gentile world, it is as *the Son of Man* that He is pictured to us, who, by His human nature, stands related as Kinsman-Redeemer to the whole race, and is therefore able and willing to save men of all nations and kindreds and peoples who turn to God through Him. Over this Gospel the words, "Behold the *Man* whose name is the Branch," may be written; while over the Gospel of John, which was designed neither for Jews nor Gentiles, neither for Greek nor Roman, but for the Church—the congregation of the faithful, those whose eyes are opened to behold His glory, "the glory as of the only-begotten of the Father, full of grace and truth"—the words, "Behold your *God*," are graven in letters of gold.

In our chapter, however, it is as the Servant that He is introduced to us by the Father—as One who is sent to accomplish a work and to fulfil a mission. And it is with special satisfaction and complacency that

God speaks of His only-begotten Son in His character as Servant. "Behold My Servant," whom I uphold; Mine elect ("My chosen One"), "*in whom My soul delighteth*"—one reason being, perhaps, because in this respect this ideal Servant stands out as the great contrast, not only to Israel nationally, who was called to be God's servant, but proved unfaithful, but to all other men. The curse of man and the cause of his ruin is pride, self-will—the striving to be independent of God, and seeking to strike out a career for himself. By seeking to be free, and thinking that freedom consists in doing, not what he ought, but what he pleases, man landed himself in bondage to sin and Satan.

But here is One who says, "Lo, I am come; in the scroll of the book it is written of Me, *I delight to do Thy will, O My God*: yea, Thy Law is within My heart," and who, when on earth, could say, "*I came down from heaven, not to do Mine own will but the will of Him that sent Me*"; "*My meat is to do the will of Him that sent Me, and to finish His work.*"

Insignficant, fallen man ever aims at exalting himself, but here is One who, though in the form of God counted not His equality with God a prize ("to be grasped" at), but emptied Himself, taking the form of a servant "and being found in fashion as a man, He humbled Himself, becoming obedient even unto death, yea, the death of the Cross." No wonder, then, that the Father points with delight to Him, saying, "Behold My Servant," and would have our eyes fixed on Him, not only as our Saviour, but as our example, that we might follow in His footsteps.

This true Servant of Jehovah, we read, "*shall deal prudently.*" The verb הִשְׂכִּיל, *his'kil,* primarily means "to act wisely," but since "wise action as a rule is also effective," and leads to prosperity, the verb is used also sometimes as a synonym for "*prosperously.*" It is used in such passages as 1 Sam. xxiii. 14, "And David was *acting wisely* in all his ways, and the Lord was with him"; and in David's charge to Solomon (1 Kings ii. 3), "And keep the charge of the Lord thy God . . . in order that thou mayest *act wisely* in all that thou doest."

In Jer. xxiii. 5, this verb is used directly of the Messiah, and describes one feature of His blessed rule, "*Behold, the days come, saith Jehovah, that I will raise unto David a righteous Branch, and a King shall reign and prosper* (his'kil, '*deal wisely*'), *and shall execute judgment and justice in the land.*" Here, in Isaiah lii. 13, it is used to describe the action of the Servant of Jehovah in relation to the great task which is entrusted to Him. "He shall 'deal wisely' and accomplish His great work *skilfully*"—an assurance, as it were, at the very outset, that "the pleasure of Jehovah shall prosper in His hand." *He shall be exalted and extolled* ("*lifted up*"), *and be very high.* There is an ancient Rabbinic Midrash on this sentence, which says, "He shall be exalted above Abraham; He shall be lifted up above Moses, and be higher than the ministering angels."

I sometimes think that when the inspired writer of the Epistle to the Hebrews sat down to write that wonderful and comprehensive treatise on the supremacy and greater glory of the Messiah, and took for his keynote the little phrase "better than,"[1] and proceeded to show how Christ was greater, and higher, and "better" than the angels, than Moses, than Joshua, than Aaron and the whole Aaronic priesthood and ritual, and than all the types and shadows of the Old Covenant, the substance and fulfilment of which are to be found in Him alone—he must have had the thought expressed in this Midrash in his mind.

Yes, our Lord Jesus is exalted above Abraham, the father of the faithful, who stands at the head of the history of the peculiar people, whose history also prefigures and unfolds the story of Redemption, inasmuch as He is not only Abraham's Son but Abraham's Lord, whose day Abraham rejoiced to see "from afar,"[2] through whom the great promise that in Abraham's seed all the families of the earth should be blessed is realized, and in and through whom the history of Abraham and of the nation which sprang from his loins receives its true significance and glory.

And "He is lifted up above Moses" because He is the Mediator of a better covenant which rests upon better promises, who brings us out of a greater bondage than that of Egypt, and whose "law of the spirit of Life" implanted in our hearts enables us to render that

---

[1] Heb. i. 4.   [2] John viii. 56.

obedience to God which the mere letter of the law graven on tablets of stone could not do.

And "He is higher than the angels, for to which of the angels did God say at any time, Sit thou on My right hand till I make thine enemies the footstool of thy feet?" which is the height of exaltation attained by the Servant of Jehovah as the Son of Man, who through the deepest sufferings enters into glory.[1]

The climax in the height of His exaltation, as set forth by the three verbs in this sentence, is expressed by the word מְאֹד, m'od, lit. *very much*, with which the sentence ends. "He shall be exalted and lifted up and be high *very much*, or exceedingly."

---

[1] "Rosenmüller observes on ver. 13*b*, 'There is no need to discuss, or even to inquire, what precise difference there is in the meaning of the separate words'; but this a very superficial remark. If we consider that '*rūm*' signifies not only to be high, but to rise up (Prov. xi. 11) and become exalted, and also to become manifest as exalted (Ps. xxi. 14), and that נִשָּׂא, *nisa*, according to the immediate and original reflective meaning of the niphal, signifies to raise one's self, whereas *gâbhah* expresses merely the condition, without the subordinate idea of activity, we obtain this chain of thought : he will rise up, he will raise himself still higher, he will stand on high. The three verbs (of which the two perfects are defined by the previous future) consequently denote the commencement, the continuation, and the result or climax of the exaltation ; and Stier is not wrong in recalling to mind the three principal steps of the *exaltatio* in the historical fulfilment, namely, the resurrection, the ascension, and the sitting down at the right hand of God. The addition of the word מְאֹד, *m'od*, shows very clearly that וְגָבַהּ, *v'gabha*, is intended to be taken as the final result ; the Servant of Jehovah, rising from stage to stage, reaches at last an immeasurable height that towers above everything besides" (Delitzsch).

Of the glorious fulfilment of it in the person of our Lord Jesus we are told in the New Testament. " *Wherefore* "—because for our salvation He descended so low, and became obedient unto death, even the death of the Cross—" *God also hath highly exalted Him* "; yes, " *far above all principality and power, and might and dominion, and every name that is named, not only in this world, but also in that which is to come.* " [1]

But after what may be called this preface of glory, which tells us at the very outset what shall be the end of His path of humiliation, the next verse of this introductory section gives a glimpse of the valley of sorrow and suffering through which the Servant of Jehovah has first to emerge—the valley which is, so to say, lengthened out and extended in the more detailed account of His sufferings in the next section. Verses 14 and 15 are in the Hebrew linked together by the words כַּאֲשֶׁר, *ka'asher*, "like," or, "just as," and כֵּן, *ken*, "so." They express, if I may so put it, the balance of proportion, and announce in advance that the effect shall be commensurable with the greatness of the cause. Let me first translate these verses literally.

" Like (or, 'just as') many were astonished at Thee (so marred, or 'disfigured,' or 'distorted' was His visage more than that of any man, and His form more than the sons of men) [2]—so shall He sprinkle many nations," etc.

---

[1] Eph. i. 20-23 ; Phil. ii. 9-11.

[2] Delitzsch renders, "So disfigured, His appearance was not human and His form not like that of the children of men " ; and Von

It is generally agreed among commentators that the words which I have enclosed in brackets must be regarded as a parenthesis and explain the reason of the astonishment at Him on the part of many. The verb שָׁמֵם, *shamem*, which is rendered "astonished," means to be desolate or waste; to be thrown by anything into a desolate or bereaved condition; to be startled, confused, as it were petrified by paralysing astonishment.[1] Even to *such an extent* will many be astonished at Him because of the greatness of His suffering, which shall cause His blessed countenance and form to be so "marred" that it shall appear, as it were, "disfigurement" itself, without any trace of the grace and beauty which belong to the human face and figure.[2]

By these strong words and expressions the Spirit of God seeks to give us a glimpse into the depth and

Orelli, "So disfigured was His visage beneath man's, and His form so unlike man's."

The sudden transition from the second to the third person is not exceptional, but is found in many other places in the prophetic writings.

[1] See its use in Lev. xxvi. 32 ; Ezek. xxvi. 16.

[2] "His appearance and His form were altogether distortion (*mishchath*, an expression stronger than *mashchath*, which means distorted—lit. away from men, out beyond men), *i.e.* a distortion that destroys all likeness to man.

"The Church before the time of Constantine, pictured to itself the Lord, as He walked on earth, as repulsive in His appearance; whereas the Church, after Constantine, pictured Him as having quite an ideal beauty. They were both right : unattractive in appearance, though not deformed, He no doubt was in the days of His flesh ; but He is ideally beautiful in His glorification. The body in which He was born of Mary was no royal form, though faith could see the *intensity* of the vicarious sufferings of our Saviour, and of the greatness of the cost of our redemption; and as we contemplate this picture of the Man of Sorrows, with the "face" which for us was "marred" more than that of any man, and with His form bowed and disfigured more than the sons of men, may our hearts be stirred with shame and sorrow for the sin which was the cause of it all, and with greater love and undying gratitude to Him who bore all this for us!

But as His humiliation and sufferings were great, yea, "more than that of any other man," so also shall the blessed fruit and consequences of them be. The fifteenth verse is, so to say, the antithesis to the fourteenth, and sets forth the state of glory after the suffering. "Like (or 'just as') many were astonished at Thee (because His visage and form were distorted by suffering 'beyond men')—so *shall He sprinkle many nations; kings shall shut their mouths at Him*" with astonishment and reverence, for that which could not "have been told them" by any man, and which was previously altogether unheard of, shall they now "see" and "understand"; or, in the words of the seventh verse of chapter xlix., which might be described as Isa. liii. in miniature, for it summarizes in few words the sufferings of the Messiah and the glory which should follow—

---

doxa shining through. It was no royal form, for the suffering of death was the portion of the Lamb of God, even from His mother's womb; but the glorified One is infinitely exalted above all the ideal of art" (Delitzsch).

"*Kings shall see and arise, princes and they shall worship,
because of Jehovah that is faithful, the Holy One of Israel
who hath chosen Thee*"—they shall see that the One
whom man humbled God has exalted; that He who
was despised of man, and abhorred of the nation, is,
after all, He whom the Holy One of Israel hath chosen;
that in spite of their vain counsels, and their individual
and united efforts, His kingdom progresses, and is
destined to triumph—and they shall "arise" from their
thrones in token of reverence, and shall signify their
submission and allegiance by prostrating themselves
before Him in worship; and all this "because of
Jehovah that is faithful" to His covenants and promises,
"even the Holy One," who will never draw back from
His word, and shall, by espousing and vindicating His
Servant's cause, make it manifest in the sight of the
whole world that He hath chosen Him!

In a measure this has already been fulfilled. Because
"He hath humbled Himself, becoming obedient unto
death, even the death of the Cross, therefore also God
hath highly exalted Him, and given unto Him the Name
which is above every name; that in the Name of Jesus
every knee should bow, of things in heaven, and things on
earth, and things under the earth, and that every tongue
should confess that Jesus Christ is Lord, to the glory of
God the Father."

Already before the crucified Nazarene kings must rise
from their thrones, and princes fall in the dust, not,
indeed, necessarily because their hearts have been sub-

dued by His grace, or their eyes opened to His essential glory as the Son of God, but because they have found out by experience that it is no longer safe to resist His power. But even though the obedience be feigned, and the worship be outward, it is still a testimony to Christ's exaltation, and to the faithfulness of Jehovah, in lifting Him out of the valley of humiliation, and appointing Him His "First-born, higher than the kings of the earth." But we are looking forward to a fuller, more visible, and universal fulfilment, when He who was "despised and rejected of men ; a man of sorrows and acquainted with grief," shall be the acknowledged King over the whole earth, and when—

" He shall have dominion from sea to sea
And from the River unto the ends of the earth.
They that dwell in the wilderness shall bow before Him ;
And His enemies shall lick the dust.
The kings of Tarshish and of the isles shall bring presents ;
The kings of Sheba and Seba shall offer gifts :
Yea, all kings shall fall down before Him ;
All nations shall serve Him" (Ps. lxxii. 8–11).

But I must return for a moment to the first sentence in this fifteenth verse, concerning which there has been much discussion. Most modern scholars object to the rendering of the word יַזֶּה, *yazzeh*, by "He shall sprinkle,', as is given in the Authorized and Revised Versions of the English Bible, and translate the phrase, "so shall He startle," or "make to tremble," or "cause to leap"—

i.e. either for joy or fear—on the ground chiefly that the parallelism between the fourteenth and fifteenth verses demands that this phrase should express "a change in those who formerly abhorred the Servant," or, as another prominent Bible scholar puts it, as a parallel to the words, "*were astonished at Thee*, we have the word *yazzeh* (which he renders, ' He shall make to *tremble*')—in other words, the effect which He produces by what He does stands over against the effect produced by what He suffers." But to this it has been replied that the real parallel (or, rather, contrast) to the words, " as many were astonished," in the fourteenth verse are the words, "*kings shall shut their mouths*," in the fifteenth verse, as is shown by the correspondence of the words, " at Thee," and "at Him " in these two sentences. I shall not enter into a minute controversial disquisition on this point, as nothing of a fundamental character really turns on it.

The priestly and atoning functions of the Servant of Jehovah stand out prominently enough in the next section of the prophecy. I will only briefly state my own grounds for retaining the rendering "sprinkle," first and chiefly because of the general usage of the Hebrew word.

The verb נָזָה, *nazah*, occurs in very many passages in the Old Testament, and the hiphil form of it, הִזָּה, *hizzah* (which is used in Isaiah lii. 15) invariably signifies "*to sprinkle*."

It is true also, as another writer observes, that

it is specially set apart and used for the sprinkling with the blood of atonement and the water of
purification.[1]

It is true that *hizzah* (to sprinkle) is usually construed with the accusative, in which case the preposition עַל, *'al*, "upon," should follow the verb. But slight
deviations and irregularities in the construction of
phrases do sometimes occur in the Hebrew Bible; they
do not, however, alter the meaning of words, and in this

---

[1] It is used, for instance, in Lev. iv. 6, xvi. 14–19, xiv. 7, Num.
xix. 19, and in many other places.

Delitzsch, who himself renders the word "He shall make to
tremble," writes: The hiphil *hizzah* (to sprinkle) generally means
to spirt or sprinkle (*adspergere*), and is applied to the sprinkling of
the blood with the finger, more especially upon the *capporeth* and
altar of incense on the Day of Atonement (differing in this respect
from *zaraq*, the swinging of the blood out of the bowl), also to the
sprinkling of the water of purification upon a leper with the bunch of
hyssop (Lev. xiv. 7), and of the ashes of the red heifer upon those
defiled through touching a corpse (Num. xix. 18); in fact, generally,
to sprinkling for the purpose of expiation and sanctification. And
Vitringa, Hengstenberg, and others, accordingly follow the Syriac
and Vulgate in adopting the rendering *adsperget* (he will sprinkle).

They have the usage of the language in their favour; and this
explanation also commends itself from a reference to נָגוּעַ (*nagua'*) in
chapter liii. 4, and נֶגַע (*nega'*) in chapter liii. 8 (words which are
generally used of leprosy, and on account of which the suffering
Messiah is called in b. Sanhedrin 98*b* by an emblematical name
adopted from the old synagogue, "the leper of Rabbi's school"),
since it yields the significant antithesis, that He who was Himself
regarded as unclean, even as a second Job, would sprinkle and
sanctify whole nations, and thus abolish the wall of partition between Israel and the heathen, and gather together into one holy
church with Israel those who had hitherto been pronounced
"unclean" (chap. lii. 1).

5

case, though *hizzah al* would mean "sprinkle upon," *hizzah* by itself still means "sprinkle," or, more properly, "besprinkle."

Secondly, the only other passage in the second half of Isaiah where another form of this same verb occurs [1] is chap. lxiii. 3, and there the word most certainly means "sprinkle." It is alleged against the rendering of the phrase, "so shall He sprinkle," that "there would be something very abrupt in the sudden representation of the Servant as priest"; but there is no more abruptness, it seems to me, in the introduction of this idea of priesthood in this passage than in the sudden transition from the exaltation described in the thirteenth verse to the depth of humiliation in the fourteenth verse.

In this introductory section we have, as stated at the beginning, a brief summary in terse, condensed form, of the whole prophecy, which is fully developed in the 53rd chapter. And to my mind it would seem strange if there were no reference also to the priestly atoning function of the Servant (of which the next section is so full), in this introductory summary.

---

[1] יַזֶּה, *v'yez*, which is Kal future, 3rd person sing. masc. of the verb נָזָה.

CHAPTER II

ISRAEL'S PENITENTIAL CONFESSION: THE HISTORY OF THE SERVANT OF JEHOVAH UNFOLDED.

THE second section, into which the whole prophecy divides itself, is, as stated above, primarily the sorrowful lament and confession of repentant Israel in the future. We are transplanted in these verses, by the spirit of prophecy, into that future solemn day of Israel's history which is described in the last chapters of Zechariah— when the spirit of grace and supplications shall be poured upon them, and their eyes shall be opened to look upon Him whom they have pierced. It is then, in the great mourning and weeping which are there described, that they shall break out with this plaintive hymn, which is musical in its sadness and betrays the agony of a broken heart and contrite spirit.

Let me say, at the beginning of this exposition, that the tenses in these verses are perfects, the future being regarded prophetically as already past. *"Who hath believed our report?"*—literally, "that which we hear," namely, the wonderful story about this glorious Servant of Jehovah, who, through His self-humiliation and vicarious suffering even unto death, has accomplished for us so great a salvation, and is now exalted to such height of glory—"*and the arm of Jehovah over (or 'upon') whom has it been revealed?*"

The arm of Jehovah is the emblem of divine power. In the 51st chapter we have the remnant of Israel appealing to it: "*Awake, awake, put on strength, O arm of Jehovah, as in the days of old, the generations of ancient times.*"[1] And in the 52nd chapter we read: "*Jehovah hath made bare His holy arm in the eyes of all the nations; and all the ends of the earth shall see the salvation of our God.*"[2]

From the context we see that it is the manifestation of this power of God in and through the Messiah that is here spoken of. "In the Servant of Jehovah who is depicted in this prophecy," an old writer truly observes, "the redeeming arm of Jehovah manifests itself: so to say, personifies itself. The Messiah Himself is, as it were, the outstretched arm of Jehovah," and the message (the proclaiming) concerning Him, "the power of God unto salvation to all who believe." But who hath believed this message? and whose eyes were opened to behold in this despised and humiliated Servant the very embodiment of the power of God and the wisdom of God? The answer implied in the first question is that *very few, if any*, did believe it; and to the second question, that only such upon whom an

---

[1] Chap. li. 9.　　　　[2] Chap. lii. 10.

operation of divine power has been performed, only those "over" or "upon" whom the arm of Jehovah has been *revealed*, could believe it—so marvellous, so utterly incredible to mere human thought and imagination is the wonderful story which, in all its saving power and glory, is now made plain to us. Truly, the message, or "report," of a full and perfect salvation through a suffering Messiah, who through humiliation and death enters into glory, could not have been known or believed, and much less invented, by either Jew or Gentile; but all the more it bears upon it the seal of Divine wisdom and Divine power. *"As it is written, Eye hath not seen, nor ear heard, neither have entered into the heart of man, the things which God hath prepared for them that love Him. But God hath revealed them unto us by His Spirit."* [1]

(1) *The Early Years and Unobtrusive Character of the Servant of Jehovah*

In the plaintive confession which follows there is incidentally unfolded also the whole earthly life-story of the Servant of Jehovah, beginning with His tender youth, which gradually develops into a manhood of suffering, and ends in a violent and ignominious death.

"For (or '*And*') *He grew up before Him as a tender plant, and as a root out of a dry ground."*

"Jehovah's Servant," as has been well said by another, "does not burst upon the world all at once in sudden

---

[1] 1 Cor. ii. 9, 10.

splendour of daring or achievement, dazzling all eyes and captivating all hearts. He conforms to God's slow, silent law of growth. This law holds in every province of God's empire. Great lives are built up under this law :—a babe on mother's lap, opening its fringed eyelids to look forth wonderingly on an unknown world; a child learning to prattle and play; a boy at school; a young man with bloom on his cheek and splendid purpose in his eye; and so onward throughout successive stages. . . . Even so did 'Jehovah's Servant' grow by a natural human growth." [1]

The word יוֹנֵק *yoneq*, translated "tender plant," literally means "suckling," but is used here figuratively (in a horticultural sense) for the tender twig upon a tree or trunk, or stalk. [2] Taken in connection with chap. xi. 1, we see that it springs up out of the decayed stump of Jesse, "after the proud cedar of the Davidic monarchy had been felled." But the second verse of Isaiah liii. presents not only a parallel but also a contrast to chapter xi. There, the figure is that of a strong, vigorous shoot coming out of the root of the decayed house of David; here, it is the frail "tender twig" or sapling, struggling out of the dry ground. Here, men are represented as turning away in disappointment, if not in disgust, from this "root" springing up out of such unpromising surroundings; there, we read in the tenth verse, "*And it shall come to pass in that day, that the root of Jesse, which standeth for an ensign of the peoples, unto*

---

[1] James Culross.   [2] Ezek. xvii. 22.

Him shall the nations seek, and His resting place shall be glory."

The difference is explained by the fact that whereas in chapter liii. it is Messiah's sufferings and rejection which are depicted, it is especially His millennial glory and reign, the beneficent effects of which extend even to the animal creation, which are described in chapter xi.

But, to return for a moment to a more minute examination of the second verse. We have here incidentally a prophetic description of our Lord Jesus during the early years of His life, concerning which there is so little recorded in the Gospel narrative. According to the manifest suggestion of the passage, "He grew up in obscurity and lowliness. Not as a prince royal, on whom the hopes and eyes of a nation are fixed, and all whose movements are chronicled in Court Gazette or Circular. Here is one living a lowly life in lowly environments. . . . Men expected 'a plant of renown,' fairer and statelier than all the trees in the garden of God, with boughs lifted cedar-like in majesty; instead, there is a suckling, a sprout from the root of a tree that had been cut down, with nothing fair or magnificent about it. It owes nothing to the soil in which it grows. The ground is dry, an arid waste without moisture; the plant is a tender one; and in that unpropitious soil whence no sweet juices can be drawn it grows up stunted, dwarfed, unattractive."

The expression "out of dry ground" (which, as

Delitzsch correctly observes, belongs to both figures, namely "tender twig," or "suckling," and "root") is intended to depict "the miserable character of the external circumstances in the midst of which the birth and growth of the Servant would take place." The "dry ground" describes the then-existing state of the enslaved and degraded nation; *i.e.* "He was subject to all the conditions inseparable from a nation that had been given up to the power of the world, and was in utter ignorance; in a word, the dry ground is the corrupt character of the age."[1]

And yet, in spite of all the obscure and adverse circumstances of His earthly environment, "*He grew up before Him*," that is, before Jehovah—"increasing in wisdom and stature and in favour with God and men," with the eye of His heavenly Father ever complacently resting upon Him.

In rendering the last part of the second verse, most modern commentators depart from the accents of the Massoretic text, and translate, "*He had no form and comeliness that we should look on Him, and no beauty that we should desire Him,*" but the English Authorized and Revised Versions properly adhere to the punctuation of the Hebrew text, and render, "*He hath no form nor comeliness; and when we shall see Him there is no beauty that we should desire Him.*"

There was nothing in His appearance or surroundings that the carnal or worldly minded could be attracted by;

---

[1] Delitzsch.

everything was so different from what they had pictured or anticipated.

It is not inconsistent with the language of the text to suppose that "there may have been in His aspect, power, grace, majesty, blended with sorrow and meekness. The heart of the thing is, that men did not see the beauty that was there; He did not answer to their ideal; He wanted the qualities which they admired; His greatness was not shaped to their thoughts. Having misread the prophecies, having imagined another Deliverer than God had promised, being blind to the heavenly, while their souls lay open to the carnal and earthly, they found nothing worth gazing upon in Jehovah's Servant when He came. They would have welcomed a plumed and mail-clad warrior, riding forth to battle against the oppressor, would have shouted before him, 'Gird thy sword upon thy thigh, O most mighty, with thy glory and with thy majesty!' They have no admiration and no welcome for One who comes, meek and lowly, to make His soul an offering for sin, and to be God's salvation to the end of the earth. It was not sin that troubled them: how should a Saviour from sin delight them? What was there in a Bringer-in of righteousness to inspire such hearts?" [1]

(2) *The Despised and Rejected of Men*

The penitential confession proceeds in the third verse to set forth the positive aversion and hostility

---

[1] Culross.

which the nation in its former ignorance manifested towards Jehovah's righteous Servant. "*He was despised and rejected* (or '*forsaken*') *of men.*"

The first description of Him in this line—נִבְזֶה, *nibhzeh*, "despised"—takes our thoughts back once more to what has already been said of Jehovah's Servant in the seventh verse of the 49th chapter: "Thus saith Jehovah, the Redeemer of Israel, and His Holy One, to Him whom man despiseth, to Him whom the nation abhorreth."[1]

If, instead of prophecy uttered centuries before His advent, it were history written subsequent to the events, no more terse or graphic description could be given of the attitude and feeling of the Jewish nation in relation to Jesus of Nazareth: "despised and rejected of men"—"whom man despiseth and the nation abhorreth."

No person in the history of the Jews has provoked such deep-seated abhorrence as He who came only to bless them, and who even on the cross prayed, "Father, forgive them, for they know not what they do." When on earth, at the end of His three-and-a-half years of blessed ministry among them, they finally rejected Him. Their hatred was intense and mysterious. "Away with this man; release unto us Barabbas. . . . Crucify Him, crucify Him!" was their cry. And all through the centuries no name has provoked such intense abhorrence among the Jews as the name of Jesus.

---

[1] Or "despised of soul," as the words in Isa. xlix. 7 may best be rendered, describing the depth of contempt, *as from the very soul of man*, which He shall encounter.

I have known personally most amiable, and as men, lovable characters among the Jews; but immediately the name "Jesus" was mentioned, a change came over their countenances, and they would fall into a passion of anger. In the course of my missionary experiences these past thirty-five or forty years, how often has it been my lot to witness some of my people almost mad with rage—clenching their fists, gnashing their teeth, and spitting on the ground at the very mention of the Name which to the believer "is as ointment poured forth"! Israel's attitude to our Lord Jesus may be gathered also from their literature. In the filthy legends about Him in the Talmud and more modern productions, the very names by which He is called are blasphemous. The precious name Yeshua ("Jesus," Saviour) has been changed into "Yeshu," made up of initial letters which mean, "Let His name and His memory be blotted out."

The Holy One who knew no sin nor was guile found in His mouth, is often styled "the Transgressor"; and another term frequently in the mouth of the Jews is "Tolui" ("the hanged one"), which is equivalent to "the accursed one." There are also other hateful designations, such as "Ben Stada," or "Ben Pandera," which imply blasphemies not only against Him, but against her who is "blessed among women."

And Israel's blind hatred to the Messiah does not stop short at His person, or His virgin mother, but extends to His words and works, and particularly to those of their nation who are ready to take upon them His reproach and to follow Him. Thus His works are still ascribed to witchcraft and Beelzebub; His gospel (the Evangelium) is called Aven or Avon-gillajon, "the sinful or mischievous writing"; while Rabbinic hatred to His followers (especially from among the Jews) was not satisfied with classing them as "apostates" and "worse than heathen," but rose to the height of instituting a daily public prayer in the most solemn part of their liturgy, that "the Nazarenes" may, together with all apostates, "be suddenly destroyed," without hope, and be "blotted out of the book of life"!

This may be painful reading to some Christians, and the Lord knows it is far from my thoughts to write anything which might tend to foster unchristian prejudice against my people, but it is necessary to show how literally the prophetic forecast has been verified, and how deep-seated and mysterious Jewish hatred has been to Him who, according to His human nature, is flesh of their flesh, and bone of their bone, and in whom is bound up all their hope and salvation.

Let it be remembered also that Jewish hatred to Christ and His followers, at any rate in more modern times, is partly to be traced to the sufferings which they have endured at the hands of so-called Christians, and also that it is not our Lord Jesus as we know Him, that Israel in ignorance thus blasphemes, but the caricature of Him as presented to them by apostate persecuting Christendom in the dark ages and since.

Often the only way left to the Jews to avenge their terrible sufferings and massacres was to write blasphemously of Him in whose name they were ignorantly perpetrated.

Neither is it to be forgotten that if Christ has been, and alas! to a large extent still is, "abhorred of the nation," there has always been a remnant in the nation to whom He has been "the fairest of ten thousand and altogether lovely," and who, for the love of Him, counted not even their lives dear unto them. It was a man of Israel and a Pharisee who wrote: "*But what things were gain to me, those I counted loss for Christ, yea, doubtless, and I count all things but loss, for the excellency of the knowledge of Christ Jesus my Lord; for whom I have suffered the loss of all things, and do count them but dung that I might win Christ.*"

And when the "blindness in part" which has befallen Israel shall be removed, and their eyes are open to behold the true glory of Him whom they have pierced, then the whole nation shall show an example of love and zeal for their Messiah, such as has not been known in the world.

The phrase חֲדַל אִישִׁים, *chadal ishim,* "rejected (or 'forsaken') of men" has been variously rendered. To quote only two or three examples, Hengstenberg translates the clause, "the most unworthy among men"; Moses Margoliouth, "the meanest of men"; and Von Orelli, "shunned of men." But it seems to me that Franz Delitzsch has caught the true force of the Hebrew

idiom. "The predicate *chadal ishim*" (rendered in the
Authorized Version "rejected of men"), he says, "is
misunderstood by nearly all the commentators, inasmuch
as they take *ishim*, the word for 'men,' as synonymous with *b'ne Adam* (children of men), whereas it is
rather used in the sense of *b'ne ish* (men of high rank,
lords) as distinguished from *b'ne Adam* (ordinary men,
or common people). Hence Cocceius explains it thus :
'wanting in men,' *i.e.* having no respectable men with
Him to support Him with their authority. In Hebrew
חָדַל, *chadal*, has not only the transitive meaning to dis-
continue or 'leave off' a thing, but the intransitive to
cease, or be in want, so that *chadal ishim* may mean one
in want of men of rank, *i.e.* finding no sympathy from
such men. The chief men of His nation who towered
above the multitude, the great men of this world,
withdrew their hands from Him : He had none of the
men of any distinction at His side."

And this, alas ! is still the case. The great, mighty,
and noble in the world, the "men of high degree" (with
few exceptions, for which God be praised), still ignore
and despise Him, and use their power and influence
to hinder rather than to advance His cause and
kingdom. It was a reproach brought against Christianity by Celsus and other early pagan writers, that
it was the religion of slaves, and Jewish Rabbis still
taunt believers from among their nation that it is to
the poor that the gospel is preached, and that those
who have been drawn to Christ belong for the most

part to "the common people." "Have any of the
rulers believed on Him, or of the Pharisees?"[1] And
not only was He "despised and forsaken," especially
by the men of high rank, the leaders of the nation,
but He was *ish-makh'obhoth vidua choli*—"a man of
sorrows" (or, "a man of pains," the Hebrew idiom
denoting "*sorrow of heart in all its forms*"), a man whose
chief distinction was that "His life was one of constant,
painful endurance"—and "acquainted" (or, "well acquainted") with grief (or, "sickness"), the meaning of
which, as Delitzsch explains, is not that He had by
nature a sickly body, falling from one disease into
another (as some would explain), but that "the wrath
instigated by sin, and the zeal of self-sacrifice,[2] burnt
like the fire of a fever in His soul and body." The
point emphasised is that sorrow and grief were the very
characteristics of the Servant of Jehovah, "the tokens
we know Him by." "We have all seen grief and
sorrow in our time," writes one; "no one can live
long without doing so, God knows; but it is not one
sorrow, or two, that makes one 'a man of sorrows,' nor
one meeting, or two, with grief that makes him the
acquaintance of it.

"How the Servant endured, with what fortitude and
patience, with what faith in God and acquiescence in
His will, is not here brought into view, but simply the
fact that sorrows came thick and heavy upon Him,
like wind-driven rain beating on an unsheltered head,

---

[1] John vii. 47, 48. [2] Ps. lxix. 9.

and that grief was present with Him as His close companion through life."

And the chief causes of His sorrows and grief were not personal ills, or physical pain, though these were great enough. It was *heart sorrow* and *grief of soul.* "A noble nature, repelled in all its efforts to bless, is pained únspeakably more by that repulse than by the crowding in of merely personal ills, or by all the slings and arrows of adversity: and His sorrow came, thus, because His brethren rejected the help He brought, repelled the Helper, and abode in their lost state."

The last two sentences in the third verse form, so to say, a *climax* in the sorrow and humiliation which the righteous Servant of Jehovah had to endure.

The words *kh'master panim mimmennu* (rendered in the Authorized Version, "we hid as it were our faces from Him") have been variously rendered. The marginal reading in the A.V. and R.V. is, "*He hid as it were His face from us,*' which is the translation adopted by Hengstenberg, who sees in it an allusion to the law in relation to the leper, who, according to Leviticus xiii. 45, had to cover his face, and cry "Unclean, unclean"; also by Margoliouth, who translates, "as one who would hide his face from us," by not revealing to us His true character and glory. But it is now pretty generally agreed among scholars that the word *master* is a verbal noun, and that the true translation is that given in the text of the English versions,

namely, "*As one from whom men hide their face*"[1] "*i.e.*
like one whose repulsive face it is impossible to endure,
so that men turn away their face or cover it with their
dress" (Delitzsch); or, as another expresses it: "Instead of meeting Him with a joyful gleam in their eyes
responding to His grace and help, men turned away
from Him—as one looks the other way to avoid the eye
of a person whom he dislikes, or as one shrinks from an
object of loathing" (Culross).

Lastly, all the predicates of shame and sorrow are
summed up in the word with which also this third verse began, נִבְזֶה, *nibhzeh*, "He was despised"—to which, however,
is added a negative preposition which the Hebrew idiom
requires to mark the *depth* of the contempt in which He
was held—"and *we esteemed Him not.*" Instead of count-
ing Him dear and worthy, we formed a very low estimate of
Him, or rather we did not estimate Him at all, or, as Luther
forcibly expresses it: "we estimated Him at nothing."

This, dear Christian reader, will be Israel's broken-
hearted confession on the day when the Spirit of grace
and supplications is poured upon them, and their eyes
are opened at last to the fearful error which they committed as a nation in the rejection of their Messiah.
But, as we read these sad and solemn words, "He was
despised, and we esteemed Him not," may we not pause
for a moment to ask ourselves if this is not true also in
professing Christendom to-day?

---

[1] A suggestive and possible rendering of the sentence also is:
"There was, as it were, a hiding of *God's* face from Him."

6

"How often," writes another Hebrew Christian brother, "do we meet Christians expatiating on the atrocious wickedness of the *Jews* in crucifying the Lord of Glory; implying, in fact, that if He had appeared amongst *them*, He would have met with a more favourable reception. There was a horrid custom once in the Christian Church, which rendered the Jews especial objects of hatred and insult during Lent, and more particularly during the ceremonies of Easter week. The Bishop used to mount the pulpit of the Cathedral, and address the people to the following effect: 'You have among you, my brethren, the descendants of the impious wretches who crucified the Lord Jesus Christ, whose Passion we are soon to commemorate. Shew yourselves animated with the spirit of your ancestors; arm yourselves with stones, assail the Jews with them, and thus, as far as in you lies, revenge the sufferings of that Saviour who redeemed you with His own blood.' Alas! this custom still prevails in some countries. You may be sure, however, that if Christ humbled Himself once more, and appeared visibly amongst us, He would be treated in the same way as He was by the Jews; yea, 'crucified afresh, and put to an open shame.' He would again have to listen to the dogmas of insolent reasoning; He would once more be disgusted with the fiend-like sneers of reprobate men, and the polished cavils of fashionable contempt." [1]

And what about ourselves, who by the grace of God

---

[1] Moses Margoliouth.

do believe on Him? Do we estimate our Lord Jesus at His true worth? Is He indeed to us the chiefest of ten thousand and altogether lovely? Are we prepared for His dear sake to forsake all and to follow Him outside the camp, esteeming the reproach of Christ greater riches than the treasures of Egypt?

(3) *The Vicarious Character of His Sufferings*

The veil lifted from their eyes, Israel sees the true cause of Messiah's sufferings, and, "bearing witness against himself, laments his former blindness to the mediatorial vicarious character of the sufferings both of soul and body that were endured by Him."[1] Oh, *it was for us*—they now say—that He endured all the shame and agony. To translate the 4th verse literally : " *Verily they were our griefs* (or '*sicknesses*') *which He bore, and our sorrows* (or '*pains*') *with which He burdened Himself, but we regarded Him as one stricken, smitten of God, and afflicted.*" No plainer or stronger words could be used to express the thought of vicarious suffering than those employed in the original of this verse.

The verb נָשָׂא, *nasa*, "to bear," is continually used in Leviticus of the expiation effected by the appointed sacrifices, as, for instance, Lev. xvi. 22, " *The goat shall bear upon him all their iniquities unto a solitary land.*" "When construed with the accusative of the sin," as Delitzsch properly explains, "' *nasa*' signifies to take the debt of sin upon oneself, and carry it as one's own, *i.e.*

---

[1] Delitzsch.

to look at it and feel it as one's own (*e.g.*, Lev. v. 1, 17), or more frequently to bear the punishment occasioned by sin, *i.e.* to make expiation for it (Lev. xx. 19, 20; xxiv. 15), and in any case in which the person bearing it is not himself the guilty person ('*nasa*' signifies) to bear sin in a *mediatorial* capacity for the purpose of making expiation for it. It is evident that both the verbs used in this verse, 'He hath borne,' and 'He carried,' are to be understood in the sense of an expiatory bearing, and not merely of taking away, as has been recently maintained in opposition to the *satisfactio vicaria*, as we may see clearly enough from Ezek. iv. 4–8, where *seth 'avon* ('bearing iniquity') is represented by the prophet in a symbolical action. But in the case before us, where it is not the sins, but 'our diseases' and 'our pains' that are the object, this mediatorial sense remains essentially the same. The meaning is not merely that the Servant of God entered into the fellowship of our sufferings, but that He took upon Himself the sufferings which we had to bear, and deserved to bear, and therefore not only took them away (as Matt. viii. 17 might make it appear), but bore them in His own person, that He might deliver us from them. But when one person takes upon himself suffering which another would have had to bear, and therefore not only endures it with him, but in his stead, this is called substitution or representation—an idea which, however unintelligible to the understanding, belongs to the actual substance of the common consciousness of man, and

the realities of the divine government of the world as
brought within the range of our experience, and one
which has continued even down to the present time to
have much greater vigour in the Jewish nation, where
it has found its true expression in sacrifice and the
kindred institutions, than in any other, at least so far as
its nationality has not been entirely annulled."

As I have already explained, in the more literal
translations of the text of the 3rd and 4th verses, the
words rendered in the English versions, "our griefs"
and "our sorrows," mean also "our sicknesses" (or
"diseases") and "our pains," and it is in this sense that
the Evangelist Matthew quotes this passage from Isa. liii.
After recording some of His precious works of healing—
how He cast out the spirits with His word, and healed
all that were sick, he adds: "that it might be fulfilled
which was spoken through Isaiah the prophet, saying,
'Himself took our infirmities and bare our diseases.'"

The question has been raised how Christ's miraculous
works of healing can be a fulfilment of this Scripture
which sets forth Messiah's *vicarious* sufferings for sinners,
and in what *sense* did He Himself "take our infirmities
and bear our sicknesses"? The answer is that these
cures were in fact and in strictness a fulfilment of this
Scripture because wrought in His character as Saviour.
As one has said: "Christ was sent for the general
purpose of *removing by the sacrifice of Himself* the evil
which sin *had brought into the world*. And this work
He commenced when He cured bodily diseases, for

these diseases were the consequences and punishment of sin. And more—they were types of another disease, of the moral and spiritual effects of man's fall, which the prophecy has principally in view, as is evident from the words which follow."[1]

To put it still more simply, the mission of the Messiah was to accomplish a full redemption for His people, and this He did not only by taking upon Himself our sins, but our "infirmities" and "diseases," which are the direct consequences of sin, though not always of the sin of the individual. The blessed results of His redeeming work to us therefore are not only pardon and regeneration, but the ultimate redemption of *body* as well as of spirit in resurrection life.

The miracles of healing not only served to certify Him as the Redeemer, and as "*signs*" of the spiritual healing which He came to bring, but were, so to say, pledges also of the ultimate full deliverance of the redeemed, not only from sin but from every evil consequence of it in body as well as in soul. Hence our full salvation includes not only the perfecting of our spirits, but the "fashioning anew of the body of our humiliation that it may be conformed to the body of His glory."

The self-accusing confession of their former blindness as to the true cause of Messiah's sufferings is continued in the second half of the verse. It was for us that He bore all this; it was our crushing burden that He took

---

[1] William De Burgh, D.D., *The Messianic Prophecies of Isaiah.*

upon Himself, they say, "*but we regarded Him as stricken* (or '*plagued*'), *smitten of God, and afflicted.*"

Every one of the three expressions, נָגוּעַ, *nagua*, "one stricken, *i.e.* afflicted with a hateful, shocking disease"— hence used particularly of "the plague" of leprosy (of which נֶגַע is, so to say, the *nomen proprium*), and מֻכֵּה־אֱלֹהִים, *mukeh Elohim*, "one smitten of God" ("one who has been defeated in conflict with God his Lord"),[1] and מְעֻנֶּה, *m'unneh*, "one *bowed down* by suffering," is intended to describe one suffering terrible punishment for sin.

The error confessed, as Hengstenberg well observes, is not in their having considered the sufferings which the Servant of Jehovah endured, as a punishment of sin, but in having considered them as the punishment *for the sins which He Himself had committed.* This, alas! is what spiritually blinded Israel has thought for all these centuries, and what most of the Jews still do think. Thus our Lord Jesus, the only sinless man who trod this earth, is called the *Poshe—the transgressor—*who, according to such illustrious exponents of the spirit of Rabbinic Judaism as Moses Maimonides,[2] well deserved the violent death which He suffered; while in the Talmud Jesus of Nazareth is placed in Hell alongside of Titus

---

[1] Delitzsch.

[2] See especially the "Iggereth Teman," the letter addressed by Maimonides to the Jewish communities in Yemen, written in Arabic in 1172, and translated into Hebrew in 1216 by Samuel Ibn Taban, now printed from a MS. in possession of the late Dr. Jellinek, Vienna, 1873.

and Balaam, and as undergoing not only the severest but the most degrading form of punishment.[1]

We can well imagine, therefore, the deep contrition and *heartbrokenness* of repentant Israel when their eyes are at last opened by the Spirit of God to the true character of this holy Sufferer, and when they perceive that it was for them and in their stead that He endured it all. "In that day" of weeping and mourning over Him whom they have pierced, we can hear, as it were, the sob which will accompany their confession: How base was our ingratitude! How intense was our ignorance! How thick our darkness! How profound our blasphemy against that Holy One, who in His love and compassion condescended to bear *our* griefs and to be laden with *our* sorrows! "Yet we regarded Him as plagued, smitten of God, and afflicted.

"*But He was wounded for our transgressions, He was bruised for our iniquities: the chastisement of our peace was upon Him; and with His stripes we are healed.*"

The וְהוּא, *v'hu* ("*and He*"), as contrasted with וַאֲנַחְנוּ, *v'anach'nu* ("*and we*") in verses 3 and 4, continue to set forth the true cause of Messiah's sufferings in contrast to our former false judgment with regard to Him. "*We*" in our former blindness and ignorance regarded Him as plagued and smitten of God for His own sin and guilt, while "*He*"—which is the emphatic word in the 5th

---

[1] Gittin, 566. The passage in the original, with translation and comment, will be found in *Jesus Christ in the Talmud*, etc., by Professors Gustave Dalman and Heinrich Laible.

verse—this Holy One, whose true glory as our Redeemer
we now behold, endured all in our stead, paying *with
His own life* for the "transgressions" and "iniquities"
which we have committed. And how great were His
sufferings, both in life and in death! He was wounded,
literally, "He was pierced through" (as the verb חלל,
chalal, primarily means)—or, "wounded to death," as
Von Orelli, and others, render it—an expression which
reminds us of Zech. xii. 10: "*They shall look upon Me
whom they have pierced,*" though the verb for piercing
used there is not exactly the same as here. And "He
was *bruised,*" literally "*crushed*" (*m'duka*), by the heavy
burden of our sin which He took upon Himself, weighted
by the wrath of God.

And it was all—to repeat once again—for *our* iniquities
and "for our transgressions." What else, we ask again,
can these words mean than that He suffered *vicariously*?
Not merely *with*, but *for* others? By no exegesis is it
possible to escape this conclusion. And there is nothing
in the conclusion that need surprise us.

"It is in keeping with what we know otherwise. You
would not abolish vicariousness by getting it eliminated
from the Bible. No one can be unfamiliar with instances of one taking upon himself the penalty of another's recklessness or folly, even within the range of
what we call 'natural law.' A child, for instance, playing
in a room beside his mother, moves a bar which he has
been forbidden to touch, and overturns a vessel of scald-
ing water. The mother sees the danger to her child,

and in an instant throws herself between him and the deadly peril, voluntarily taking upon herself her child's penalty, and saving his life at the cost of cruel suffering for herself. Cases less or more resembling this are not uncommon within the range of ordinary observation.

"To leave out vicarious suffering were to erase the brightest pages from the story of the past,—of all golden deeds,—of men who have died for their country,—of martyrs who have gone to stake or scaffold for the truth's sake, and helped to pay the purchase-price of our religious light and freedom; and would leave history but a poor record of ignoble selfishness or mean ambition, a record unutterably sad, little better than the record of a herd of wolves or a Newgate Calendar. Seldom, indeed, has there been love absolutely pure from the taint of selfish feeling; and yet it has been strong enough to take upon itself much suffering in the stead of others; and has taught us at least to acknowledge that it is a sweeter thing to do good than to enjoy selfish ease and pleasure, a nobler thing to suffer for others than to win the world's renown.

"Among the Jews, the idea of vicarious suffering was far from strange; their sacrificial system distinctly expressed it. Sin (said the sacrificial system) is an offence unspeakably odious to God, which He cannot look upon, but must punish. Death is the due punishment of sin. But God has no pleasure in the sinner's death. He is full of mercy, and has Himself opened up a channel, through sacrifice, whereby sin may be expiated, and pardon granted in righteousness. The sacrifices under the law had no intrinsic efficacy to put away sin; but only symbolized substitution—the substitution of Jehovah's righteous Servant in place of the guilty. Men may indeed exclaim against the propriety of one suffering for others, and may insist that every man be wounded for his own transgressions and bruised for his own iniquities. But there is no moral reason, so far as I can see, to forbid love from voluntarily stepping in and suffering for others, to save them from badness and misery. Now in this prophecy, here is One suffering for sins which He never committed—enduring what others deserved—standing in the transgressor's place, as if Himself the transgressor.

"Within the human bosom, the world over, are self-accusings and poignant regrets because of ill that has been done, and dread of what may be, when God shall reckon with us. The case may not be clear to the man himself; but the sense of guilt is there, ineradicable;— it is done; I did it; I cannot undo it; no tears or re-pentings can change the fact; and I dread the future, for I hear a Voice which proclaims with mysterious, awful sovereign authority, 'Woe unto the wicked; it shall be ill with him.' And so the conscience of the sinner is in a condition of pain, varying from mere uneasiness to darkest and intensest remorse.

"A fire smoulders within that may blaze up any hour into fierce misery. Under such conditions, there can be no true peace with God, no true love to Him, no true joy in Him, no true walking before Him; but revolt and aversion whenever His will thwarts and crosses ours.

"Oh, if only that guilty past were blotted out and made as if it had never been! Oh, if only I could go forward into that unknown future a pardoned man! But the question of blotting out that guilty past is not so simple as at first it seems.

"The forgiveness of sins is a question of righteousness as truly as of mercy. If God cannot forgive in righteousness, then He cannot forgive at all. If He were to forgive simply because He is compassionate, or because (being sovereign) He so wills it, or out of mere good nature, He would remove the very ground on which my conscience plants itself in all its moral operations. It behoves that the glory of His character and the rectitude of His government should suffer no eclipse, but, on the contrary, be demonstrated. But now light is thrown on the case—though still deep mystery remains—when it is said, 'The chastisement of our peace was *upon Him.*' Through His suffering for others, they obtain 'peace,' in the sense of reconcilement to God."[1]

The phrase *musar sh'lomenu*—the "chastisement (or punishment) of our peace"—denotes "the chastisement which leads to our peace," or, as more fully expressed by Von Orelli, "The punishment of our well-being—*i.e.* by the bearing of which, on His part, our peace or well-being is secured — *was upon Him,*" *i.e.* He bore the burden of it in our stead. The same thought is differ-

---

[1] Culross.

ently expressed in the last supplementary clause in this verse: "*By His stripes*" (*ubhachabhuratho*, literally His wounds) "*we were healed* (or, *healing was brought to us*)."[1] Peace and healing—two most blessed results which accrue to us from the vicarious suffering and atoning death of our Saviour.   Peace *with God* because of His *justifying* grace on the ground of what Messiah bore and did for us ; and peace in our own conscience, which can never be at peace until sin is expiated—and "healing." This, I believe, goes beyond justification, and hints at the regenerating, *sanctifying* grace in the souls of the justified, for the work of our Saviour not only procures pardon and reconciliation with God, but is the ground also of the work of the Holy Spirit, who accomplishes *within us* His mission of renewal and sanctification, so that, delivered from spiritual disease and moral blemish, we may become conformed to His own image.

(4) *The Moral Necessity of Messiah's Sufferings*

The 6th verse, as is well observed by Dr. J. A. Alexander, describes the occasion, or rather the *necessity*, of the sufferings of the Servant of Jehovah, which are spoken of in the verses which precede : "*All we like sheep have gone astray ; we have turned every one to his own way, and Jehovah hath laid* (literally, '*caused to meet*') *upon*

---

[1] חַבּוּרָה, *chabhurah*, denoting a tumour raised by scourging. Margoliouth translates the clause, "By reason of His contusions we were healed." In Isa. i. 6 *chabhurah* is rendered "bruises" in the English Version. It may well lead our thoughts to the cruel scourging endured by our Saviour on our behalf.

Him the iniquity of us all." It is because men are
wholly estranged from God, and an atonement was required for their reconciliation, that Messiah suffered and
died. "As the sea furnishes a thousand illustrations
of life or truth to the 'inhabiters of the isles,' so the
shepherd and the flock to the Hebrew prophets and
psalmists. The picture is that of the scattered flock,
all wandering from the pasture and the protection and
care of the shepherd. It is not, as in the parable, the
wandering of one sheep out of a hundred, ninety-and-
nine being left, but the scattering of the whole flock.
Under this figure is represented *our iniquity*, the word
implying both the sinful act and its guilt. Sheep are
not to blame for wandering; they know no better; but
in men, with reason, conscience, and heavenly light,
wandering means sin." [1]

Thus, to repeat, "*we all*," without any exception, are
involved in this sin and guilt and consequent misery of
having strayed from the Great Shepherd, who is Himself
also the fountain of life and all blessedness. But while
"the sinful alienation is *universal*, the modes of its
manifestation are as various as men and their tendencies."
"We have turned every one," [2] or, more literally, each

---

[1] Culross.

[2] "The second clause is understood by Augustine as denoting
selfishness, and a defect of public spirit, or benevolence; and this
interpretation is admitted by Hengstenberg as correct 'if taken in
a deeper sense,' viz. that union among men can only spring from
their common union with God. But this idea, however just it may
be in itself, is wholly out of place in a comparison with scattered

(one) man, " to his own way," which is the very opposite
of the way of God. "We have turned," so that we are
not only involved in the sin of the mass, but stand also
under a load of personal and individual guilt which we
have incurred. But let us not forget that it is primarily
still the penitential confession of the remnant of Israel,
and the special applicability of the figure employed in
this verse to the nation, which, because they have
wandered away from God, have for many centuries
been a scattered flock, and as sheep having no shepherd.

"Any one taking a view of the state of the Jewish
nation, both spiritual and temporal, since they rejected
their Messiah," writes a Hebrew Christian brother,
"cannot fail to be struck with the graphic description
in this concise inspired sentence. ' *We have each one
of us turned to his own way*.' We have all gone in
the path which *we* chose. There was no union in the
service of God; no common bond to unite us; we have
not entered into the thoughts of God, nor endeavoured
to follow His ways, but we went on the broad way of our
own. We were like sheep which are scattered; which
have no shepherd, which wander where they please, with

---

sheep, whose running off in different directions does not spring
from selfishness, but from confusion, ignorance, and incapacity to
choose the right path. A much better exposition of the figure,
though still too limited, is that of Theodoret, who understands it
to denote the vast variety of false religions, as exemplified by the
different idols worshipped in Egypt, Phœnicia, Scythia, and Greece,
alike in nothing but the common error of departure from the true
God " (J. A. Alexander).

no one to collect, defend, or guide them. One would wander in one direction, and another in another; and of course solitary and unprotected, they would be exposed to the more danger. Such has been the state of the Jewish nation since they have rejected the Lord of Glory; they have been sifted among all nations like as corn is sifted, and everywhere they turn to their own way; they have neither king, nor prince, nor sacrifice, nor Ephod."

Disunion among themselves as well as corporate wandering from God has marked their history in dispersion. But to return to the more immediate context: while ours was the sin and guilt, Jehovah, in infinite grace and mercy, "*laid* (or more literally, *caused to meet*, or *caused to alight*[1]) *upon Him the iniquity of us all.*"

עָוֹן, *avon* ("iniquity"), is used to denote not only the transgression itself, but also the guilt incurred thereby, and the *punishment* to which it gives rise. The last word, *kullanu*, translated "of us all," is the very same also with which this verse began, rendered "all we." It

---

[1] הִפְגִּיעַ, *hiph'gia'*, from פָּגַע, *paga'*, signifies to cause anything to strike, or fall upon a person. The rendering in the English Version ("laid upon Him") is objectionable only because it is too weak and suggests the idea of mild and inoffensive gesture, whereas that conveyed by the Hebrew word is necessarily a *violent* one, namely, that of "causing to strike, or fall" (Alexander). The verb is used in such a passage as 2 Sam. i. 15: "Go near and *fall upon him*; and he smote him that he died." "In other passages our iniquity is spoken of as resting on the Holy One, and He bearing it. Here it is spoken of as coming upon Him like a destroying foe and overwhelming Him with the wrath that it brought with it" (B. W. Newton).

is repeated to give emphasis that it is the sin of "all we," primarily of all redeemed Israel, but inclusively also of all the redeemed from among all the nations, yea, of every individual sinner, who in repentance and faith turns to God, for as "all we" are included in the sin and guilt, so also are we all included in the provision of God's redeeming grace.

And it is Jehovah Himself who caused "all this great multitude of sins, and mass of guilt, and 'weight of punishment,'[1] to light upon Him." The previous verses have shown man's guilty hand in the case, now we must mark Jehovah's action. *He* it was who placed this awful burden on His shoulders. This was at once His deepest humiliation and His most glorious distinction.[2] "There is a striking antithesis in this verse," writes one. "In *ourselves* we are scattered"—"astray"—"each one turned to his own way"; in *Christ Jesus* we are collected together. By nature we wander and are driven headlong towards destruction; in Christ we find the way by which we are led to the gate of life. Yes, *Jehovah hath caused to meet in Him the iniquity of us all.* He was the object on which all the rays collected on the focal point, fell. These fiery rays which would have fallen on all mankind diverged from divine justice to the east, west, north, and south, were deflected from them and converged in Him. So the Lord caused to meet in Him the punishment due to the iniquity of *all.* How wonderful are God's judgments![3]

---

[1] Delitzsch.   [2] Culross.   [3] Margoliouth.

7

(5) *The Voluntary Character of His Sufferings*

But while men, in their ignorance of His true character, "and with wicked hands," heaped humiliations and sufferings upon Him, and Jehovah Himself "laid upon Him the iniquity of us all," the righteous Servant of Jehovah endured all the shame and sorrow *voluntarily*. This is set forth in the next three verses, which describe the manner of Messiah's vicarious life and death and burial.

There has been much discussion over the first part of the seventh verse, and quite a number of different renderings have been suggested by the commentators. The Authorized Version reads:

"*He was oppressed, and He was afflicted; and He opened not His mouth*," which the Revised Version has altered to, "*He was oppressed, yet when He was afflicted He opened not His mouth.*"

Delitzsch translates, "He was ill-treated, whilst He bowed Himself," *i.e.* "suffered voluntarily"; and Von Orelli, "He was used violently, though He humbled Himself." To these I may add the rendering given by Bishop Lowth, which is the same as already suggested by Cyril (among ancient writers) and by De Dieu, Tremellius, and others, namely: "*It was exacted*, and He was made answerable, and He opened not His mouth."

This last rendering comes, according to my judgment, nearer to the true sense of the original, but while נִגַּשׂ, *niggas* (rendered in the English versions, "He was

oppressed") does indeed mean to *exact*, and may here
be used in the *impersonal* sense, the rendering of the
second verb (נַעֲנֶה, *na'aneh*) by "He was made answerable"
is not in accord with its usage in the original, for the
word nowhere else conveys the notion of legal responsi-
bility. Margoliouth, on the ground that נִגַּשׂ, *niggas*, is
sometimes applied to the *rigorous* exaction of *debts*, paraphrases the first part of the verse thus:

"*He was rigorously demanded to pay the debt, and He
submitted Himself, and did not open His mouth.*"

That the Messiah in His love and compassion for
man became our surety and took upon Himself our
great moral debt, paying the ransom with His own life,
is a truth set forth in the whole of this great prophecy,
even if it be not fully expressed in this particular
sentence. What this passage does emphasize is that
He "bowed Himself" under this heavy burden, which
He took upon our account *voluntarily*. "He was
oppressed," "He was used violently," "He was treated
tyrannically" (which is yet another suggested meaning
of the word *niggas*), and *He*—which is the emphatic
word in the verse—"He Himself" it was who "bowed,"
or "humbled," or "submitted" Himself, and opened
not His mouth.

This voluntary endurance is in the second half of the
verse set forth in a simile: "*As a sheep that is led to
the slaughter,*" and "*As a lamb before its shearers is dumb,
and opened not His mouth.*"

"The object of the whole passage is to mark the

meek and quiet subjection of our Redeemer in His prolonged suffering. He was the subject of cruel and
unjust oppression, yet His persecutors were not crushed.
God allowed them to pursue their course and to accumu-
late sorrows on the head of the Holy One; and He
patiently and meekly bowed His head to the infliction,
and opened not His mouth."[1]   " When *we* suffer," writes
one, "how hard we find it to be still! The flames of
resentment—how they leap up in our bosom, and flush
our cheek with angry red! What impatience there often
is, what murmuring, what outcry, what publishing of our
sorrow! Or if there is silence, it is at times akin to
stoicism, the proud determination not to let men see
how we feel. But the spirit of the Servant is loftier and
grander unutterably. In sublime and magnanimous
silence He endures to the uttermost, sustained by His
mighty purpose and by the conviction, *Jehovah wills it.*
I see the temper of His mind in this silence ; I see His
strength; I see His rest in God; and I look down
into the unfathomed mystery of Love. He came to do
what only Love was equal to—that is abundantly clear—
and He shrank from no suffering; raised not His arm,
opened not His mouth, in His own defence, wearied
not, fainted not, but was dumb with silence."[2]

But we may, I believe, go a step further. In this
wonderful patience and silence of the Servant—which in
the history of fulfilment was exhibited in the silence of
our Lord Jesus before the Jewish Sanhedrin and before

---

[1] B. W. Newton.   [2] Culross.

the Roman Procurator, Pontius Pilate—we see not only
His lamb-like meekness and "His love for man, which
made Him content to suffer for our redemption," but
His acquiescence in the justice of God in the punishment
of sin, the whole burden of which He bore. To the
Christian this verse is specially precious because of the
prominence given to it in the New Testament. Not
only was it "from this Scripture" that the evangelist
Philip "preached Jesus" unto the Ethiopian eunuch;
and not only does the Apostle Peter use it as the basis of
his exhortation to believers to be patient in suffering
and to follow the example of Him, "who when He was
reviled, reviled not again, and when He suffered He
threatened not, but committed Himself to Him that
judgeth righteously"; but, as Delitzsch truly observes,
"All the references in the New Testament to the Lamb
of God (with which the corresponding allusions to the
Passover are interwoven) *spring from this passage in the
book of Isaiah.*"

(6) *The Trial and Death of the Servant of Jehovah*

We now come to perhaps the most difficult verse
in this great prophecy, the main purport of which is to
describe the closing portion of the life of the Servant of
Jehovah and the manner of death that He should die.

"No three words in the Hebrew Bible (with the exception perhaps of the four words which follow) have been
more variously rendered," says Dr. Henderson, than those
which constitute the first sentence in this eighth verse.

It would not be to much profit were we to enter into
examination of the many translations and paraphrases of
these three words in ancient and modern versions and
commentaries.   The Authorized Version reads, "*He
was taken from prison and from judgment*," and the
Revised Version, "*By oppression and judgment was He
taken away*."   A suggestive reading, first given by Dr.
Henderson, and adopted by Margoliouth, is : "*Without
restraint and without a sentence He was taken away*,"
which of course fits in with the fulfilment of the prophecy
in our Lord Jesus, who exercised no manner of restraint
over His persecutors, and was given over to a cruel
death in violation of every principle of justice, and
without a proper trial or sentence.   But this, though a
possible and suggestive rendering, does somewhat strain
the meaning of the words from their general usage.   On
the whole, I prefer the reading given by Delitzsch, Von
Orelli, and others: "*He was taken away from prison
and from judgment*," which is almost, though not quite,
the same as that in the Authorized Version.   The
principal emphasis (in the sentence) is not laid upon the
fact that He was taken away from suffering, but that it
was *out of the midst* of suffering that He was carried off.

The idea that is most prominent in the word לֻקָּח,
luqqach ("taken away"), is that of being snatched or
hurried away.[1]   The word עֹצֶר, *otser* (rendered "prison"),
primarily means a violent constraint.   "Here, as in
Ps. cvii. 39, it signifies a persecuting treatment which

---

[1] See, *e.g.*, chap. lii. 5; Ezek. xxxiii. 4.

restrains by outward force, such as that of prison or bonds. . . . The word *mishpat* ('judgment') refers to the judicial proceedings, in which He was put upon His trial, accused and convicted as worthy of death—in other words, to His unjust judgment . . . Hostile oppression and judicial persecution were the circumstances out of which He was carried away by death."[1]

The second sentence in this verse, consisting of the four words וְאֶת דּוֹרוֹ מִי יְשׂוֹחֵחַ *V'eth doro mi y'soche-ach*, has also been very variously rendered and interpreted by translators and commentators.

The Authorized Version reads : "*And who shall declare His generation ?*"

The Revised Version connects the sentence with the words that follow, and translates : "*And as for His generation, who among them considereth that He was cut off from the land of the living for the transgression of My people ?*" etc., which is practically the same as that given by Delitzsch and others. Von Orelli translates : "*And among His contemporaries who was concerned.*"

Of other suggested renderings I may mention the following :—

(1) "*As to His generation, who shall set it forth ?*" *i.e.*, in all the guilt of their iniquity.

(2) "Who shall declare His life ?" *i.e.* the mystery of His Being.

(3) "Who can declare the number of His generation ?"—*i.e.* of those inspired by His spirit or filled with

---

[1] Delitzsch.

His life.[1] Luther, Calvin, and Vitringa understand the
clause to mean, "Who can declare the length of His
life hereafter?"; Kimchi, like Hengstenberg, explains
it to mean, "Who can declare His posterity?" Yet
another rendering based on the fact that דוֹר (*dor*) sometimes stands for "habitation," or "dwelling," is that
given by Hoffmann and Margoliouth, namely, "As for His
dwelling, who cares for it?" (or who can speak of it?)[2]

This great variety of opinions by Bible scholars, both
ancient and modern, Jewish and Christian, will give the
reader an idea of the difficulty of coming to a positive
conclusion as to the actual meaning of this clause, and
how unbecoming it would be to speak with anything like
dogmatism. Yet I may venture to suggest an explanation which seems to me the most probable. In the
Hebrew Bible דוֹר (*dor* rendered "generation") signifies
"an age," or "the men living in a particular age"; or, in
an ethical sense "the entire body of those who are
connected together by similarity of disposition," or likeness of moral character.

The Pillel verb שׂוֹחֵחַ, *soche'-ach* (rendered in A.V.
"declare," and in R.V. "considereth"), signifies, "a
thoughtful consideration," "meditation,"[3] but it means
also "to speak," "to complain," "to lament," and is

---

[1] Hengstenberg.

[2] See Isa. xxxviii. 12, R.V. The new American Jewish translation of the Bible renders: "And with His generation, who did
reason?"

[3] *E.g.* Ps. cxliii. 5, "I remember the days of old, I *meditate*
(שׂוֹחֵחַ, *soche'-ach*) on all Thy doings."

used in at least one or two places to describe an exercise
very much akin to *prayer*. As, for instance, Ps. lv. 17,
" Evening, morning, and at noonday *will I pray*, and cry
aloud : and He shall hear my voice." The words " will
I pray" (the R.V. has, " will I complain") are a translation of this same verb.[1]   I would therefore translate
" As for His generation—who (among them) poureth
out a complaint?" (*i.e.* at His treatment); or, " who
among them uttereth a prayer?" (*i.e.* on His behalf). In
either case there may be, as suggested already by Bishop
Lowth, a prophetic allusion to the custom which prevailed among the Jews in the case of trials for life to call
upon all who had anything to say in favour of the accused,
to come and " declare it," or " plead " on his behalf.

The following striking passage from the Talmud
(Sanhedrin fol. 43) may be cited by way of illustration.
" There is a tradition : On the eve of the Sabbath and
the Passover they hung Jesus. And the herald went
forth before him for forty days crying, ' Jesus goeth to
be executed, because he has practised sorcery and
seduced Israel and estranged them from God. Let
any one who can bring forward any justifying plea for
him come and give information concerning it; but no
justifying plea was found for him, and so he was hung
on the eve of the Sabbath and the Passover. Ulla said,
' But doest thou think that he belongs to those for

---

[1] As a noun it is found also in the inscription of Ps. cii.—a
prayer of the afflicted when he is overwhelmed and poureth out his
complaint (שׂיחו, *sicho*) before Jehovah.

whom a justifying plea is to be sought? He was a very seducer, and the All-merciful has said, Thou shalt not spare him, nor conceal him.' But the case of Jesus stood differently because he stood near to the Kingdom": or as others translate, "for his place was near those in power."

That this legend about Jesus has for its basis a well-known custom in the procedure of the Sanhedrin in trials for life, there is, I think, no doubt; [1] for the principle by which they were supposed to be regulated was that "they sat to justify, and not to condemn; to save life, and not to destroy." That this humane custom of calling upon those who knew anything in favour of the accused to come and declare it, was not observed in the case of Jesus of Nazareth, and that the proceedings at this hasty, *mock* trial before the Sanhedrin were in flagrant contradiction with the regulations which were supposed to govern their procedure, are facts of history, but there is this much truth in this Talmudic passage, that none *dared* to appear in His favour; and that in the great crisis when the Christ of God stood on His trial before the corrupt hostile Jewish hierarchy and the representatives of the then great Gentile world power, no one came forward with a justifying plea "on His behalf" for fear of the Jews. Yea, at that solemn

---

[1] Lowth thinks that our Lord referred to this custom in His words to the high priest in John xviii. 20, 21, "I spoke openly to the world. . . . Why askest thou Me? ask them that have heard Me," etc.

moment, when the sword awoke to smite the Shepherd, the sheep were all scattered; and even His own disciples, who later on when convinced of His resurrection became as bold as lions, and willingly laid down their lives for Him, became demoralized with fear and forsook Him and fled.

And in a sense our Lord Jesus is still on His trial. Are we, His professed disciples, ready now to take our stand as His witnesses in the face of a hostile Jewish and Gentile world, and make our "justifying plea" on His behalf not only in word but by showing forth the power of His gospel over our own hearts and lives?

But this has been somewhat of a digression. The next clause in this verse proclaims clearly the *fact* of His death, and the manner of it. "*For He was cut off out of the land of the living.*" It is by wicked and violent hands that this righteous Servant of Jehovah dies —"*cut off*," as it were, in the midst of His days. And then, finally, in repudiation once again of their previous false notion that it was for His own sin that He was "stricken and smitten of God" (ver. 4), the *vicarious atoning* character of His sufferings and death is yet again emphasized: "For the *transgression of My people the stroke fell upon Him.*"

Ewald, one of the chief fathers of the German rationalistic school of interpreters, who assigns a different (and earlier) authorship for 53rd chapter than the rest of the writings of the Great Unknown,[1] with which,

---

[1] The name with which the critics have christened their "second Isaiah."

according to him, it has somehow become incorporated,
adduces the "frequent repetition of expressions and
ideas which occur nowhere else " in the second part of
Isaiah, as a ground of his theory; but these "frequent
repetitions," as Dr. Alexander observes, "so far from
being rhetorical defects, or indications of another
author, are used with an obvious design, namely, that of
making it impossible for any ingenuity or learning to
eliminate the doctrine of vicarious atonement from
this passage by presenting it so often, and in forms
so varied and yet still the same, that he who succeeds
in expelling it from one place is compelled to meet
it in another. Thus in this verse, which fills up
the last particulars of the humiliation and sufferings
of the Messiah even unto death, it is once again
repeated that it was *"for the transgression of My
people"* that the stroke fell upon Him.

As already pointed out in the introductory part, the
term עַמִּי, *Ammi* ("My people "), can only apply to Israel,
and is one of the many internal marks which make it
impossible to interpret the prophecy of the Jews as a
nation, for the servant *suffers* and dies *for* the people,
and therefore cannot be confounded *with the people*.
Yes, the Good Shepherd laid down His life in the first
instance for *"My people"*—the people which in a
special sense He calls " His own," and that is the chief
ground of our hope and confidence for Israel *as a
nation*, but, blessed be God! He died, not for the
nation only, but that " He might also gather into one the

children of God that were scattered abroad"; [1] and since Christ came, in whom this prophecy received its minute fulfilment, millions from among all the Gentile nations, "who in time past were no people," are now the people of God. [2]

(7) *God's Special Interposition in the Burial of His Servant*

The prophetic story of the Servant of Jehovah unfolded in this penitential confession moves on. From

[1] John xi. 51, 52.

[2] No little controversy has centred round the last line of this verse. It is contended by Jewish controversialists that לָמוֹ, *lamo* (the last word in the verse which I have rendered "upon Him"), has the plural suffix and ought to be translated "upon them," and this is adduced by some in proof that it is a *collective* subject that the prophet speaks of in this chapter, namely, Israel.

But first Kimchi, who originated this argument, himself denied it. In his commentary he says: "I should like to ask the Nazarenes who explain the Parashah of Jesus, how the prophet could have said *to them* (לָמוֹ) when he ought to have said "to him" (לוֹ), for לָמוֹ (*lamo*) is plural, being equivalent to לָהֶם (*la-hem*)." But in his grammar he says: "מוֹ (*mo*) occurs as the affix of the 3rd person singular, as in Job xx. 23; xxii. 2." And again, "מוֹ (*mo*) *is used both of many and of one*." There are also other instances in the Hebrew Bible besides these two passages in Job quoted by Kimchi where the poetic plural suffix לָמוֹ is used for the singular. We find it even in this second part of Isaiah, chap. xliv. 15—"he maketh it a graven image, and falleth down thereto" (לָמוֹ). But even if it be admitted that *lamo* is here a plural, there would be no ground for the assertion that the subject is a collective one. The translation would then be: "For He was cut off from the land of the living. For the transgression of My people—the stroke or punishment that should have fallen on them." This is admitted in the New American Jewish translation of the Bible, which renders: "*For the transgression of My people, to whom the stroke was due.*"

His life of vicarious suffering and atoning death we come to His *burial.*

> "*And they made (or 'appointed'*[1]*) His grave with
> the wicked,
> And with a rich man in His death,
> Because He hath done no violence,
> Neither was deceit in His mouth.*"

"The predictions concerning Christ in this chapter," writes Moses Margoliouth, "are so numerous and so minute that they could not possibly have been dictated by any but by Him to whom all things are naked and open, and who worketh all things according to the counsel of His own will. The most *insignificant* circumstances connected with our Lord's death are set forth with as much accuracy as those which are most important. If we reflect but for a moment on the peculiar circumstances which attended our Saviour's last hours, we shall see reason to exclaim with Moses, "The secret things belong unto the Lord our God"; or with Paul, "O the depth of the riches both of the wisdom and the knowledge of God! how unsearchable are His judgments, and His ways past finding out!" What could be more unlikely than that the Messiah should be crucified when crucifixion was not a Jewish but a Roman punishment? And yet David (in Ps. xxii.) predicted that such would be the case centuries

---

[1] וַיִּתֵּן, *vayyitten* (rendered in Authorized Version "He gave"), is, as generally admitted, used here, as in many other places in the Hebrew Bible, impersonally, as in the German *man gab.*

before Rome was founded. Again, the fulfilment of David's prediction was brought about by the Jews themselves *contrary to their own law and tradition*. The law expressly forbade to choose a heathen for their king, for the following are the words of Moses, whose disciples they averred they were: " *Thou shalt in any wise set him king over thee whom the Lord thy God shall choose; and from among thy brethren shalt thou set a king over thee: thou mayest not set a stranger over thee, which is not thy brother.*" [1]

Their *Rabbinic* law pronounced the most severe *anathema* against any one who should deliver a Jew to a heathen magistrate. But in *this* case—that the word of God may come to pass—they regard neither their law nor their tradition, but deliver Jesus to the judgment of the Roman Procurator and call upon him to pronounce sentence. And when Pilate, half in remonstrance and half in mockery, said: "Shall I crucify your King?" they replied, "We have no king but Cæsar."

After the remarkable fulfilment of an extraordinary prophecy when Jesus was really put to death according to the *Roman* law, and was crucified between two male-factors, what more likely than that He should be treated as they were? But no: for when Pilate, yielding once more to the clamour of the Jews that the death of the victims should be hastened so that the bodies should not remain on the cross on the Sabbath—" *The soldiers*

---

[1] Deut. xvii. 14, 15.

came and broke the legs of the first and of the other that
were crucified with Him ; but when they came to Jesus
and saw that He was dead already, they broke not His
legs.　Howbeit one of the soldiers with a spear pierced His
side, and straightway there came out blood and water. . .
These things came to pass that the scriptures might be
fulfilled, a bone of Him shall not be broken—and again
another scripture, They shall look upon Him whom they
have pierced."　Again, "what more insignificant than that
the soldiers should *part His garments* and *cast lots for
His vesture*?　Yet that too, with a great number of
other incidents equally minute, was circumstantially
predicted." [1]　And so also was it with His burial.

The Jewish leaders, not content with the humiliations
and sufferings they heaped upon Him ; not appeased
even by the cruel and shameful death to which at their
will He was given over, followed Him with hatred even
to the grave.　"*They appointed His grave with the
wicked.*"

"In all countries, I suppose, it has been the rule that
persons put to death as criminals have had ignominious
sepulture," writes one.　"Even after death shame has
followed them, though after ages have ofttimes reversed
the award and built monuments to them."　But this
was especially the case among the Jews.　This was the
law of the time, as stated by Josephus.[2]　"He that blas-

---

[1] Margoliouth.　I have taken the liberty to abbreviate and slightly
recast his remarks.

[2] *Antiquities*, IV. viii. 6.

phemeth God let him be stoned, and let him hang upon a tree all that day, and let him be buried in an ignominious and obscure manner." Now, it was as a blasphemer that they condemned Him in their ignorance and blindness, and what more likely than that as He died with criminals He should also be buried with them ? *But—"with a rich man (He was) in His death."* [1]

Modern scholars have sought to explain the word עָשִׁיר, *'ashir,* as being a synonymous parallel to רְשָׁעִים, *r'sha'im* (" wicked "), in the previous clause. This explanation is, as far as I can trace it, first mentioned by Rabbi Sh'lomoh ben Melekh of Fez in his Mikhlol Yophi (about 1500 A.D.), where he says, " 'Ashir (rich) is

---

[1] The word for death is in the plural, and some have argued that it should be rendered, "in His deaths," and have adduced it as yet another proof that the subject of the prophecy is a collective one. But there is no basis for this assertion, for first, if a plurality of persons were intended, it is the *plural suffix* which would be required, and this is here expressed by the singular. "There is no ground," as Pusey correctly observes, "to lay any emphasis on the plural in מֵתִים, *methim* 'death,' than חַיִּים, *chayyim* 'life' (in the preceding verse), which is also in the plural—the singular for 'life' not being used in Hebrew. Many nouns in Hebrew are used in the plural where we Westerns could hardly account for it. The plural is used of *a condition* as a period of life, or a condition of body. There is then no reason why מֵתִים, 'deaths,' if there is any stress on the plural, should not mean 'the state of death,' as חַיִּים, *chayyim* (the plural for 'life,' the state of life)."

In Ezek. xxviii. 10 "deaths" is certainly used "for the death of one." Delitzsch says the plural is used of a violent death, the very pain of which makes it like dying again and again.

8

considered by Rabbi Yonah to be equivalent to *rasha'*, 'wicked'"; but he himself adds that "it is not allowable to abandon the usual signification '*rich*' merely on account of the parallel clause."

This explanation, which Franz Delitzsch properly says, is "untenable," has unfortunately been adopted by Luther, Calvin, and Gesenius, who regard the word "rich" here as suggesting the necessary idea of "one *who sets his heart* upon his wealth, or puts his trust in it," or makes an unlawful use of it. But this is so arbitrary that some of the later writers abandon the Hebrew usage altogether, and profess to derive the sense "wicked" from an Arabic root. But this, as Dr. Alexander truly says, "is *doubly* untenable; first, because the Hebrew usage cannot be put aside for an Arabic analogy without extreme necessity, which does not here exist; and secondly, because the best authorities (as Delitzsch also shows) find no such meaning in the particular Arabic word itself.[1]

It may seem surprising that this forced imposition of a new and foreign meaning on a word so familiar should be thus insisted on. "Luther and Calvin, no doubt, simply followed the rabbinical tradition; but the later writers have a deeper motive for pursuing a course which, in other circumstances, they would boldly charge

---

[1] Ewald, Hoffmann, Böttcher, etc., have tried their hands at altering the original word so as to produce a synonymous parallelism to "wicked," but this is a violent method of handling the sacred text, especially when there is absolutely no necessity for it.

upon the Reformer's ignorance of Hebrew. That motive is the wish to do away with the remarkable coincidence between the circumstances of our Saviour's burial and the language of this verse, as it has been commonly understood since Capellus" (Alexander).

And this "remarkable coincidence" is truly wonderful, for, in the words of Delitzsch, "if we reflect that the Jewish rulers would have given to Jesus the same dishonourable burial as to the two thieves, but that the Roman authorities handed over the body to Joseph the Arimathæan, a 'rich man' (Matt. xxvii. 57), who placed it in the sepulchre in his own garden, we see an agreement at once between the gospel history and the prophetic words, which could only be the work of the God of both the prophecy and its fulfilment, inasmuch as no suspicion could possibly arise of there having been any human design of bringing the former into conformity with the latter."

And the reason assigned for this honourable burial, which was so different from what had been planned, or "appointed" for Him by His enemies, is that—"*He hath done no violence, neither was deceit found in His mouth*"—which is yet another reiteration of the absolute innocence of His outward actions and of the inward purity and gentleness of His character. It was *vicarious* sufferings that He endured; it was a death of *atonement* for others that He died; but immediately those sufferings were ended and that death accomplished, *His humiliation was ended*, and no further indignity to His blessed person could be permitted.   And so, already, in His burial, He was "separated from sinners," and was laid in the tomb of the " rich man of Arimathæa, wherein never man before was laid." [1]

[1] Luke xxiii. 53.

CHAPTER III

THE RESURRECTION AND FUTURE GLORY OF
THE SERVANT OF JEHOVAH

WITH the 10th verse begins the account of the Messiah's exaltation and glory. But first it is once more reiterated and emphasized that they were not mere chance experiences which the Servant of Jehovah passed through. Nor was it merely that wicked men were allowed to work out the evil of their hearts in the sufferings and humiliations which they were permitted to heap upon Him, and thus make manifest by their treatment of "the Holy One" their enmity towards God.

No: "the supreme *causa efficiens*," as Delitzsch expresses it, was God, "who made the sin of men subservient to His pleasure, His will, and predetermined counsel."

"*Yet it pleased Jehovah to bruise* (דַּכְּאוֹ, *dak'o*, literally *to crush*) *Him; He hath put Him to grief.*" [1]

---

[1] הֶחֱלִי, *he'cheli*, as is generally admitted by scholars, is the hiphil of חָלָה, *chalah*. Both the verbs "to bruise," or "crush," and "to put to grief," or "afflict with sickness," go back to verses 4 and 5: "He hath borne our griefs," or "sicknesses," and "He was bruised," or "crushed," "for our iniquities."

This is the confession of the penitents whose eyes are now opened to see the true meaning of it all. He who "had done no violence nor was deceit found in His mouth," "whose actions were invariably prompted by pure love, and whose speech consisted of unclouded sincerity and truth," was yet "crushed" and put to grief by Jehovah. "Here is not only the mystery of suffering innocence; but of innocence suffering at the hands of righteousness and perfect love." Yes, mystery of mysteries; and apart from the explanation He Himself gives of it, it is the most inexplicable thing in God's moral government. But it is fully explained, not only in all that preceded in this chapter, but by the great purpose of redemption formed by the triune God before the world was founded, and which is progressively unfolded in the pages of the Old and New Testaments.

In this light of God's own revelation the sufferings of the Messiah in which the good pleasure of God's will was accomplished, become a mystery of light in which there is no darkness at all. We see that this pleasure of Jehovah in the sufferings of the Righteous One, to use the words of another, "does not proceed from caprice, but that He acted righteously as well as sovereignly in what He did.

"Not only did the Lord bruise Him, but it was the 'good pleasure of His will' to do so. He who has no pleasure in the death of the wicked was pleased to put His righteous Servant to grief—not, of course, because the death-agony was a pleasure to look upon, but as means to the fulfilment of a great purpose.

"Even a noble-minded man finds pleasure in contemplating heroic and self-sacrificing love in others, to accomplish glorious ends. We look back, for example, on our martyrs, who suffered cruel death for the Gospel's sake; we forget the physical torture they endured; or rather it ceases to be a horror in our eyes, and becomes a glory; we read of their sufferings with uplifted and joyful hearts, thanking God who gave such grace to men. And even so, we cannot help thinking, the Lord, whose pity is like unto a father's pity, had pleasure in the self-sacrifice of His Servant; yea, had pleasure in the very appointment which issued in the self-sacrifice. And if we add to this — as exhibited in what follows — the results which the sufferings achieved, in their nature, blissfulness, magnitude, and perpetuity, we shall understand how it comes to be said, 'Yet it pleased the Lord to bruise Him: He did put Him to grief.'"[1]

These blessed results the spirit of prophecy in the mouth of the penitent confessors now proceeds to enumerate, after emphasizing yet again that they are all conditioned on His sufferings and death.

"*If* (or *when*), *His soul shall make an offering for sin.*"

The word תָּשִׂים, *tasim* ("shall make"), is either second person masculine, in which case the rendering would be as in the Authorized and Revised Versions, "When Thou (*i.e.* God) shalt make His soul an offering for sin";

---

[1] Culross.

or third person feminine, " When His soul shall make an
offering," which is the rendering accepted in the margin
and by most modern scholars. The latter translation is
preferable, as Jehovah is nowhere else addressed in this
chapter. In either case the Servant of Jehovah gives
His life as an offering for the sin of others and takes
on Himself the penalty which their guilt had incurred.
" Language could not more simply and unequivocally
declare the significance of His death."

The word rendered " offering for sin " אָשָׁם, *asham*,
really means " trespass," but just as the word חַטָּאת
chattath, which is used for " sin offering," " denotes first the
sin, then the punishment of the sin, and the expiation of
the sin, and hence the sacrifice which cancels the sin ;
so *asham* signifies first the guilt or debt, then the
compensation or penance, and hence the sacrifice which
discharges the debt or guilt and sets the man free."
There was much in common between the trespass
offering and the " sin offering." Both are called *kodesh-
kadashim*, " most holy,"[1] and as regards the manner in
which the sacrifice was to be slain, and as to which
portions were to be burnt on the altar, and what parts
assigned to the priests, there was " one law for them
both."[2]

Yet there were differences between the *chattath* (sin
offering) and *asham* (trespass offering), and in their
moral and typical significance each one of the sacrifices
set forth a distinctive aspect of the great work of atone-

---

[1] Lev. vi. 17 ; xiv. 13.   [2] Lev. vii. 7.

ment which was to be accomplished by the Messiah[1] and the blessed results accruing therefrom to sinful men. On the whole, it is correct to say with Dr. Culross, that while the sin offering looked to the sinful state of the offerer, the trespass offering was appointed to meet *actual transgressions*, the fruit of the sinful state. The sin offering set forth propitiation, the trespass offering set forth satisfaction. It was brought by the transgressor "to make amends for the harm that he hath done." "It symbolized rights violated and compensation rendered, debt contracted and satisfaction made." But whether it be a sin offering or a trespass offering it had to be *slain*, and its blood shed before it could become a *sacrifice*.

I. The first of the blessed results of Messiah's vicarious sufferings and atoning death which are enumerated in this 10th verse is expressed in the two Hebrew words, יִרְאֶה זֶרַע, *yir'eh zera'*, " *He shall see His* (or more literally a) *seed* (or *posterity*)." Jewish controversialists, supported by some Gentile rationalistic writers, have based a quibble on this clause. Taking *zera'*, " seed," in its literal sense as denoting natural offspring, they have

---

[1] " Every species of sacrifice had its own primary idea. The fundamental idea of the *'olah* (burnt offering) was *oblatio*, or the offering of worship ; that of the *sh'lamin* (peace offering) *conciliatio*, or the knitting of fellowship ; that of the *minchah* (meat offering) *donatio*, or sanctifying consecration ; that of the *chattath* (sin offering) *expiatio*, or atonement ; that of the *asham* (trespass offering) *mulkta* (*satisfactio*), or a compensatory payment. The self-sacrifice of the Servant of Jehovah may be presented under all these points of view. It is the complete antitype, the truth, the object, and the end of all the sacrifices " (Franz Delitzsch).

argued that this prophecy cannot apply to Jesus of Nazareth, who had no natural progeny, overlooking the fact that this "seed" (like the other fruits of His atoning Passion set forth in the last three verses of the prophecy) follows His death, on which it is conditioned, and therefore cannot be taken in a literal sense.[1]   No; the Messiah's "seed," of which the spirit of prophecy speaks here, is the glorious *spiritual* progeny which He has begotten with "the travail of His soul," and the new family which He came to found, and which sprang, so to say, at His resurrection out of His empty tomb, is the new "seed of Israel," or the Household of Faith. This spiritual "seed"—the "bringing of many sons unto glory"[2]—was the chief joy which was set before Him, for the sake of which He endured the cross, despising the shame.   Except a grain of wheat fall into the ground and die, it abideth alone; but if it die, it beareth much fruit; and the Church of Christ, consisting of the multitude of the redeemed out of all nations, Jew and Gentile—which was born when He died, and which looks back to Him as the source of its life and the origin of its being— is the continuous living witness to this truth.

The parallel scripture to Isa. liii. is Ps. xxii. There also the sufferings of the Messiah are minutely foretold in advance as well as the glory which should follow.

---

[1] זֶרַע, *zera'*, is again and again used in the Hebrew Scriptures in a figurative sense of spiritual seed.   It is used also in this sense of spiritual "seed," or disciples, in post-Biblical Rabbinical writings.

[2] Heb. ii. 10.

And among the blessed results which are there set forth as following from His death is, "*A seed (zera')* *shall serve Him*";[1] which shows that it is not a literal but a spiritual seed, namely, His disciples, or followers, who also "serve" Him.

II. "*He shall prolong His days.*" How wonderful, how seemingly paradoxical! He "pours out His soul unto death," as a trespass offering; He is "cut off from the land of the living"; is dead and buried, and yet He shall live and have continuance of days!

How is it possible? The answer to this question is that the Messiah was not only to die for our sins but must rise again from the dead "according to the Scriptures." And in the light of the glorious fulfilment all these seeming paradoxes in the Old Testament in reference to the person and mission of the Messiah are cleared up.

Our Lord Jesus, who was delivered up for our offences, was raised again for our justification, and ascended into heaven, where He now sitteth at the right hand of God, whence His word of encouragement and assurance comes to His disciples: "*Fear not, I am the First and the Last, and the Living One; and I became dead, and behold I am alive for evermore, and have the keys of death and of Hades.*"[2]

This prediction that Messiah shall "prolong His days" after having died, is in accord also with what we read in other Scriptures, as for instance Ps. xvi. 10: "*Thou wilt not leave my soul in* (or *to*) *Sheol; neither*

---

[1] Ps. xxii. 30.   [2] Rev. i. 17, 18.

wilt Thou suffer Thine Holy One to see corruption"; and
Ps. xxi. : "*He asked life of Thee, Thou gavest it Him,
even length of days for ever and ever,*" which Jonathan
in his Targum, and Kimchi in his Commentary, themselves explain that the expression *orekh yamim,* "*length
of days,*" refers to "the life of the world to come," and
so in fact it must be, since it is for ever and ever.

III. "*And the pleasure of Jehovah shall prosper in
His hand,*" *i.e.* God's will shall be fully accomplished
by Him : the mission on which He is sent He shall
triumphantly carry through.   But if we want to know
more particularly what this "pleasure of Jehovah" is,
which is thus to be brought to prosperous issue "in
His hand," we find the answer in the commission
entrusted to the perfect Servant of Jehovah as set forth
in this second part of Isaiah.   Let me quote only two
or three passages from preceding chapters.

"*Behold My Servant, whom I uphold ; My chosen, in
whom My soul delighteth : I have put My Spirit upon
Him, He shall bring forth judgment* (or "*justice*") *to the
nations. . . . I Jehovah have called Thee in righteousness,
and will hold Thy right hand, and will keep Thee and
give Thee for a covenant of the people, for a light of the
Gentiles ; to open the blind eyes, to bring out the prisoners
from the dungeon, and them that sit in darkness out of the
prison house.*"   "*And now, saith Jehovah that formed Me
from the womb to be His Servant, to bring Jacob again to
Him, and that Israel be gathered unto Him: . . . yea,
He saith, It is too light a thing that Thou shouldest be*

*My Servant to raise up the tribes of Jacob, and to restore
the preserved of Israel: I will also give Thee for a light
to the Gentiles, that Thou mayest be My salvation unto
the end of the earth."* [1]

This then, in brief, is the pleasure of Jehovah which
shall prosper in His hand, or be brought to a triumphant
accomplishment through His mediation, namely, the re-
gathering of Israel, the bringing back of Jacob, not only
to his land but into new covenant relationship with God,
of which He Himself will be the bond; the illumination
of the Gentile world with the light of the knowledge of
the true and living God; the establishing of judgment
and justice in the earth; the deliverance of men from
spiritual blindness and the bondage of sin, and the
bringing near of God's salvation to all men throughout
the whole world, even "unto the end of the earth."

And to this we must add words from the New Testament which open up yet more illimitable vistas of this
"good pleasure" of Jehovah which is to be realized in
and through the mediation of the Messiah. *"For it was
the good pleasure of the Father,"* writes the Apostle Paul,
*"that in Him should all the fulness dwell; and through
Him to reconcile all things unto Himself, having made
peace through the blood of the cross . . . whether things
upon the earth or things in heaven."* And again,
*"Making known unto us the mystery of His will according
to His good pleasure, which He purposed in Him unto a
dispensation of the fulness of times, to sum up all things*

---

[1] Isa. xlii. 1–7 ; xlix. 5, 6.

in Christ, the things in the heavens, and the things upon the earth . . . according to the purpose of Him who worketh all things after the counsel of His will."[1] "Glorious consummation of redemption," exclaims one, "which is also the manifestation in its fulness of the Divine Love!"

---

[1] Col. i. 19, 20 ; Eph. i. 9–11.

CHAPTER IV

*JEHOVAH'S FINAL WORD CONCERNING HIS
SERVANT—THE GLORIOUS AWARD FOR
HIS SUFFERINGS.*

In the last two verses "the prophecy leaves the standpoint of Israel's retrospective acknowledgment of the
long-rejected Servant of Jehovah, and becomes once
more the prophetic organ of God Himself, who acknow-
ledges the Servant as His own."[1] In this climax God
puts, so to say, His own seal to the penitent confession
of repentant Israel, and sets forth once again the
glorious results of the vicarious sufferings and atoning
death of His righteous Servant.

"*He shall see of the travail of His soul*" (or, more
literally, "because," or, "in consequence of the toil or
labour of His soul), He shall see and be satisfied."
This "travail of soul" includes, as has been well
observed, "all the toil, suffering, and sorrow through
which He came, and has been outlined, if not unfolded,
in the previous part of the prophecy. It culminated
when He was cut off out of the land of the living, and
His soul was made an offering for sin, accomplishing

---

[1] Delitzsch.

what the Levitical sacrifices only symbolized. No
accumulation of mere bodily sufferings could satisfy
these expressions. The 'travail' is that of the soul;
it has its seat within, and is such as might find voice
in those words reported from Gethsemane, 'My soul is
exceeding sorrowful. even unto death,' or in those
other words reported from the cross, 'My God, My
God, why hast Thou forsaken Me?' It is what the
Greek litany calls 'unknown agonies.'" [1]

But what is it that He shall see, *i.e.* look upon with
delight, and be abundantly satisfied? [2] For answer we
have, I believe, to go back to the verse which immediately
precedes as well as to what follows.

Abarbonel, followed by some Christian commentators,
paraphrases, "He shall see, *i.e.* His seed; He shall be
satisfied, *i.e.* with length of days." That is true, but it
goes beyond and includes the full and final accomplishment of all "the pleasure of Jehovah." In part this is
already being realized. He who for us men and our
salvation endured agony and shame, and poured out
His soul unto death, is now seated at the right hand of
God, being endowed as the Son of Man with "length of
days for ever and ever," and everywhere He beholds with
joy " a seed that serveth Him."

---

[1] Culross.

[2] The verb יִשְׂבָּע, *yisba'* = from. שָׂבַע, *sabha'*, means not only to be
contented, but to be *filled*, or abundantly supplied. It stands for
the fullest realization of expectation, or gratification of any particular
desire.

Then, apart also from the multitude which no man can number, who have been redeemed by His precious blood and who out of love for Him have sought to do the will of His Father in heaven, the *indirect* influences of His gospel in almost all parts of the earth have been great and wonderful. But this is not all for which Christ suffered and died. This is not all the " pleasure of Jehovah," which He came to accomplish. It is only when Redemption is fully completed that " He shall see " a glorious completed church " without spot or wrinkle "; a restored and converted Israel which shall bear upon itself the inscription " Holiness unto Jehovah," and be " the priests of Jehovah " and the willing " ministers " or God in diffusing the blessings of their Messiah's gospel among all nations ; a world which shall be " filled with the knowledge of God as the waters cover the sea "; and a new heaven and a new earth wherein shall dwell righteousness for evermore. Yes, He shall see all this as the outcome of the travail of His soul, *and be satisfied*.

One of the most blessed results of the "travail of His soul," and that which at the same time forms no little part of the " satisfaction " for all the sufferings which He endured, is the prerogative with which He is endowed of removing guilt and imparting righteousness to those who, through faith in Him, seek communion with God.

" *By His knowledge shall My righteous Servant justify many*," or, to give a more literal rendering of the words

9

in the order in which they stand in the Hebrew, "*By His knowledge shall make righteous* (or, *bring righteousness*) *the Righteous One* (*My Servant*) *many.*"

It cannot be positively stated whether בְּדַעְתּוֹ *beda'to* (by His knowledge), is to be understood in a subjective sense of the Servant of Jehovah, *i.e.* "according to His knowledge," or objectively, "by the knowledge of Him." Grammatically it might be rendered either way, but it is correct to say with Delitzsch (who himself favours the subjective view) that nearly all the commentators who understand by the Servant of Jehovah the divine Redeemer, give preference to the latter of the two explanations, namely, *by the knowledge of Him on the part of others.* And this, it seems to me, is the more satisfactory view. The kind of "knowledge" expressed in the word is not only that which has reference to understanding with the mind, but a practical, experimental knowledge [1] —a spiritual *heart* acquaintance with Him, a personal appropriation by a living faith of His redeeming work for sinners—such a "knowledge," for instance, as is implied in the words of Christ, "This is life eternal, *that they might know Thee* the only true God, and Jesus Christ whom Thou didst send," or, in the prayer of the Apostle, "*That I might know* Him and the power of His resurrection."

The construction of the phrase צַדִּיק עַבְדִּי, *Tsaddiq 'abhdi*, is unusual, and is intended to emphasize the unique character of the Servant of Jehovah and to explain

---

[1] יָדַע, *yada*, stands in the Bible for *experimental* knowledge.

in part *how it is* that He is the bringer of righteousness to others.

"It is in the Hebrew language as a rule, that the adjective should be placed *after* the substantive to which it belongs. But in the passage before us that rule is transgressed. 'Righteous' is not placed after 'Servant,' but stands before it, and that without the article. The omission of the article before words which are, nevertheless, definite, indicates both in Hebrew and Greek that the person or thing denoted is to be regarded as standing in a sphere of its own—singular, isolated, or pre-eminent. So it is here. We must translate 'One that is righteous, or 'the Righteous One.' The omission of the article indicates that the person thus spoken of held in earth a position of righteousness that was singular and isolated, and that there was none like it. The peculiar position of the word 'righteous' preceding, and not following its substantive, is intended to give especial prominence to the thought it expresses. Our minds are intended to rest on the righteousness of the Righteous One as the procuring cause of the blessing spoken of in this verse. In virtue of having been the Righteous One, He becomes the causer, or bringer of righteousness to His believing people.

"Yet whilst prominence is thus given to the great fact of His righteousness, it is important also to observe that the words '*My Servant*' are added. . . .

"It is not in virtue of that essential righteousness that pertains to Him as God—one with the Father and the

Holy Ghost—that He brings to us righteousness. The righteousness by which we are constituted righteous is a *service*, an *obedience* which He became man in order to render, and which He commenced and finished *in the earth*. It commenced when He said, "Lo, I come to do Thy will, O God." It terminated when He had become obedient unto death, even the death of the cross, and said, "It is finished." It is true, indeed, that unless He had been one to whom righteousness essentially belonged, He could not have wrought out the righteousness which He did work out as the Servant. The service of that Servant had in it a superhuman excellency, for that Servant was Immanuel—God manifest in the flesh. "[1]

The word יַצְדִּיק, *yats'dik*, followed as it is by the preposition לְ, *le*, ought, as I have already suggested, to be rendered "shall cause, or bring righteousness."

The רַבִּים, *rabbim* ("many"), to whom He thus brings righteousness, or constitutes righteous, is the mass of mankind, or all—not only in Israel, but amongst the nations also—who shall respond to His call, and by a living faith enter into an acquaintance with Him. It is probable that this passage was in the mind of our Saviour when, on the night of His betrayal, He took the cup and said to His disciples, "This is my blood of the New Covenant which is poured out *for many* (τὸ περὶ πολλῶν[2]), and it is almost certain that it was in the mind of the Apostle Paul when writing Romans v. 12–21,

---

[1] B. W. Newton.　　　　[2] Matt. xxvi. 28.

which is an inspired unfolding and application of the same doctrine of substitution which is set forth in this great Old Testament prophecy. After writing of the consequence of Adam's transgression to the whole of mankind, he says : "*But not as the trespass, so also is the free gift. For if by the trespass of the one the many be dead, much more did the grace of God, and the gift by the grace of the one man, Jesus Christ, abound unto many. . . . For as through the one man's disobedience the many were made sinners, even so through the obedience of the One shall the many (οἱ πολλοί), be made righteous.*" To repeat, it is the righteousness of faith which is the consequence of justification on the ground of the atoning work of the Messiah which is set forth in this passage, yet those are not altogether wrong who maintain that it *includes also* that "righteousness of life which springs by an inward necessity out of those sanctifying powers that are bound up with the atoning work which we have made our own."[1] For though this is not the ground of our acceptance before God, it is yet important to remember that the doctrine of justification does not stand alone in the Bible, and that God does not constitute any one righteous to whom He does not also impart the power *to be* righteous. We are justified that we may also be sanctified and glorified, and the outward seal of the true followers of Christ is that they "depart from iniquity" and "walk not after the flesh, but after the Spirit." But to return to our immediate context. "Because our

---

[1] Delitzsch.

righteousness has its roots in the forgiveness of sins as an absolutely unmerited gift of grace without works, the prophecy returns once more from the justifying work of the Servant of Jehovah to His sin-expunging work as the basis of all righteousness."

"*And their iniquities He shall bear.*" The introduction of the pronoun, as Dr. Alexander observes, makes a virtual antithesis suggesting the idea of exchange or mutual substitution. *They* shall receive His righteousness, and *He* shall bear the heavy burden[1] of their iniquities. "From this doctrine the heart that is self-righteous, hard, and proud may turn scornfully away— as Naaman did when told to dip seven times in Jordan; but to the man who knows himself to be a ruined and helpless sinner, and who has been made to sigh for reconcilement and peace with God, the news of grace to the ill-deserving manifested in righteousness will be welcome beyond all thought, and mighty to produce newness of life."[2]

Before we pass on to the last verse let me quote also a note by Delitzsch on this last clause: "This *yisbol* (He shall bear)," he says, "which stands along with future verbs, and being also future itself, refers to something to be done by the Servant of Jehovah after the completion of the work to which He is called in this life, and denotes the

---

[1] The thought expressed in יִסְבֹּל, *yisbol*—"shall bear"—is that of pressure as of a heavy burden. It is the future of the same verb as is rendered "carried" in ver. 4.

[2] Culross.

continued operation of His ' bearing,' or ' carrying ' (ver. 4)
through His own active mediation. His continued lading
of our trespasses upon Himself is merely the constant
pressure and presentation of His atonement which has
been offered once for all. The dead yet living One,
because of His one self-sacrifice, is an eternal Priest, who
now lives to distribute the blessings that He has acquired."

The last verse takes us back, as it were, to the very
beginning of this prophecy (chap. lii. 13-15), and sets
forth again the personal exaltation of the One who has
been despised and rejected of men, and the victor's
prize, which He shall receive on His triumphant emer-
gence from the conflict with the powers of darkness.

" *Therefore will I divide (or ' allot') to Him a portion
among (or ' in') the many (or ' great'), and with the
strong shall He divide the spoil.*"[1] The award is be-
stowed upon Him by Jehovah's own hand—" *I will
divide Him a portion* "—and the prize is glorious beyond
conception, for the *rabbim*, "many," who form His
portion include not only " His own " nation, whom He
saves and blesses, and who shall yet render Him such

---

[1] The Septuagint and Vulgate, followed by the Fathers and many
modern commentators, render בָּרַבִּים (*barabbim*), among the many,
and אֶת־עֲצוּמִים (*eth-atzumim*), with the strong, as accusatives, and
explain "the great" and "the strong" as constituting the spoil
given to the Servant of Jehovah. But the more natural construction
of the words is that given in the English versions. בְּ (*be*) occurs
nowhere else as a connective of this verb with its object, and the
particle, אֶת (*eth*), must mean *with*, as it is indeed rendered in this
same verse, where it occurs again, as well as in the ninth verse.

loyal devotion and service as the world has not known, but extends beyond the bounds of Israel to the Gentile nations.

"What is meant by His having His portion among the *rabbim* (the 'many,' or 'great')" observes Delitzsch, "is clearly seen from such passages as chaps. lii. 15 and xlix. 7, according to which the great ones of the earth will be brought to do homage to Him, or, at all events, to submit to Him." But this is only a mere outline. For the full extent of His "portion" as the Son of David and Son of Man, who, in order to carry out the pleasure of Jehovah in the redemption of the world, took upon Himself the form of a servant, we have to go to a Scripture like the 2nd Psalm: "Ask of Me, and I will give Thee the heathen for Thine inheritance, and the uttermost parts of the earth for Thy possession"; or Psalm lxxii. :

"He shall have dominion also from sea to sea.

And from the River unto the ends of the earth.

They that dwell in the wilderness shall bow before Him ;

And His enemies shall lick the dust.

   .   .   .   .

Yea, all kings shall fall down before Him :

All nations shall serve Him."

But while His portion is "divided" or allotted to Him of God, He Himself "divides spoil" "with" or "among" the strong. These עֲצוּמִים (*atsumim*, "strong" or "mighty ones") are those who flock to His banner

and go forth with Him to the conflict against the powers
of darkness.   They are those of whom we read in the
third verse of the 110th Psalm : " Thy people offer themselves willingly (or 'are all willingness,' or 'thorough
devotion') in the day of Thy power."   They are those
whom the beloved John beheld in vision as " the armies
of heaven," following in His train as He rides forth in
glorious majesty, conquering and to conquer, "riding
upon white horses, clothed in fine linen, white and pure." [1]

With these He condescends to share His triumph and
to divide the spoil taken from the enemy by making
them partners with Himself in His kingdom and glory,
even as they were sharers in His sufferings.   And truly
He and no one else is worthy to be thus exalted, and
deserves the glorious award which God bestows upon
Him.   This is emphasized in the recapitulation of His
peerless merit in the last words of this wonderful
prophecy.

" *Because He poured out His soul unto death, and was
numbered with the transgressors.   And He* (*Himself*)
*bore the sin of many.   And He made intercession for the
transgressors.*"

The phrase תַּחַת אֲשֶׁר, *taḥath asher*, expresses more
distinctly than the English rendering "because" the
idea of compensation or reward.   It has been translated
by some "instead of," or "*in return for that, i.e.* the
glorious portion or allotment which is divided to Him
by the Father is 'in return' for the great Redemption

---

[1] Rev. xix. 14.

which He has accomplished with His own life's blood. The word הֶעֱרָה, *he'erah* (rendered 'poured out'), means 'to strip,' 'lay bare,' 'empty,' or to 'pour clean out,' even to the very last remnant."[1] And it was "His soul," which stands here for *His life-blood*, which He thus *completely* emptied out "unto death."

And although all this was in accord with the predeterminate counsel of God, He did it *voluntarily*, for this also is implied in the original verb, which accords again with His own word, which has already been quoted: "*Therefore doth My Father love Me, because I lay down My life. . . . No man taketh it from Me, but I lay it down Myself.*" And not only did He thus voluntarily pour out His soul unto death as an atonement for sinners, but "*He was numbered*" (or, as Delitzsch, Hengstenberg, and others more properly translate the reflexive verb נִמְנָה, *nim'nah*, He suffered Himself, *i.e.* voluntarily, to be numbered, or "reckoned") "*with transgressors,*" פֹּשְׁעִים, *posh'im*—that is, not only ordinary sinners, such as all men are, but *criminals*—open transgressors of the laws of God and of man, with whom to be associated would be a great humiliation for ordinary men, and how much more to the "Holy One." To the believer it is precious and interesting to remember that this clause formed one of the direct quotations from this chapter made by our Lord Jesus Himself just before His betrayal and crucifixion. "This which is written," He said, "must be fulfilled in Me, And He was

---

[1] Delitzsch.

reckoned among transgressors."[1] It was, indeed, as another writer observes, "one of those remarkable coincidences which were brought about by Providence between the prophecies and the circumstances of our Saviour's passion"[2] that the Christ should have been crucified between "two thieves" (or, more literally, "*robbers*"), but this one striking incident did not exhaust the scope of the prophetic word.

He suffered Himself also to be reckoned with transgressors "in the judgment of His countrymen, and in the unjust judgment (or 'sentence') by which He was delivered up to death as a wicked apostate and transgressor of the law."[3] "And *He*"—the pronoun is *emphatic*—"*He Himself bare the sin of many*"—blessed words which are again and again joyously echoed in the New Testament, as, for instance, in 1 Pet. ii. 24: "*Who His own self bare*" (or "carried up") "*our sins in His own body upon the tree, that we, having died unto sin, might live unto righteousness*"; and Heb. ix. 26–28, where there is also an underlying allusion to the great Old Testament prophecy: "*But now once at the end of the ages hath He been manifested to put away sin by the sacrifice of Himself. And inasmuch as it is appointed unto men once to die, and after death the judgment: so Christ also, having been once offered to bear the sins of many, shall appear a second time, apart from sin, to them that wait for Him unto salvation.*"

---

[1] Luke xxii. 37.   [2] J. A. Alexander.
[3] Delitzsch.

Yes, He Himself, the Holy One, who knew no sin, bare our sin right "up to the tree," and "was made sin for us," enduring the penalty due to it on our behalf, that we might for ever be freed from the accursed load and "become the righteousness of God in Him."

The whole prophetic picture of the sufferings of the Messiah and of the glory that should follow closes with a brief but pregnant reference to His priestly function :

"*And He made (or 'maketh') intercession for the transgressors.*"

The verb יַפְגִּיעַ, *yaph'gia'* ("made intercession"), is an instance of the imperfect or indefinite future, and expresses a work begun, but not yet ended. Its most striking fulfilment, as Delitzsch observes, was the prayer of the crucified Saviour, "Father, forgive them, for they know not what they do." But this work of intercession which He began on the cross He still continues at the right hand of God, where He is now seated, a Prince and a Saviour, to give repentance unto Israel and the forgiveness of sins. Wherefore also He is able to save to the uttermost (or "completely," "all along") them that draw near unto God through Him, "*seeing He ever liveth to make intercession for them.*" Hence also the triumphant challenge of the Apostle, " *Who shall lay anything to the charge of God's elect? It is God that justifieth. Who is He that condemneth? It is Christ Jesus that died, yea, rather that was raised from the dead, who is at the right hand of God, who also maketh intercession for us.*"

But remember, dear Christian reader, that He who is
now our Advocate (or blessed *Paraclete*) with the Father,
by whose unceasing priestly ministry in the heavenly
sanctuary our life of fellowship with God is maintained,
bears also "His own" nation Israel on His heart.
It was for them primarily that He prayed on the cross.
And now at God's right hand He still pleads for them,
"*For Zion's sake will I not hold My peace,*" He says,
"*and for Jerusalem's sake will I not rest, until her
righteousness go forth as brightness and her salvation as a
lamp that burneth*"—because it is not till then that the
glory of Jehovah shall fill this earth as the waters cover
the sea, and our Lord Jesus Christ shall see of the
travail of His soul and be satisfied. Will you not for
love of Him share in this ministry of intercession for
the people which, in spite of all their sins and apostasies,
are still beloved for the fathers' sakes, and whose
receiving again into God's favour will be as life from
the dead to the whole world?

"I have set watchmen upon thy walls, O Jerusalem;
they shall never hold their peace day nor night. Ye
that are Jehovah's remembrancers, take ye no rest, and
give Him no rest till He establish and till He make
Jerusalem a praise in the earth."

APPENDIX

THE SUFFERING MESSIAH OF
THE SYNAGOGUE [1]

THE TARGUM

THE oldest testimony we possess that Isa. liii. was by
the Synagogue applied to the Messiah is found in the
Targum on the Prophets ascribed to Jonathan ben
Uzziel (first century, A.D.). Although the Targum in
the form we now possess it has been edited in Babylonia
in the fourth century A.D., yet there is no doubt that

---

[1] After the MS. of this little work was already completed I asked
my friend and fellow-worker in the Hebrew Christian Testimony
to Israel, Mr. J. I. Landsman, to copy for me a few of the most
striking passages from the Talmud and Midrashim which speak of
a suffering Messiah, thinking it might interest Christian readers if
they were added as an appendix.

Mr. Landsman has kindly done more than I asked, for some of
the passages are, as will be observed, already either quoted or
alluded to in the first part of this book.

I think it well, however, to give the whole of his collection here,
as these extracts (most of which he has translated from the original
sources) represent in orderly form the different sections of Rabbinic
literature, and follow in chronological sequence.

the material it contains is derived from sources more
ancient, and that as a whole it is of Palestinian origin.
The paraphrase—for it is not a literal translation—of
the chapter begins with the words:

> "Behold my servant, the Messiah, shall prosper;
> He shall be high, and increase, and be exceedingly
> strong."

This is almost a literal translation. But in what
follows the Targum, though ascribing to the Messiah a
central place in Israel's redemption, contrives by a
method singularly strange to us to make Israel the real
sufferer, naturally at the hands of the Gentiles, but for
her own sins, the modern Jewish idea of Israel suffering
for the sins of the nations being entirely foreign to the
Targum. In this way the Targum succeeds in purging the
Messiah from any taint of personal suffering and humiliation. Verses 3 and 4 are therefore thus paraphrased:

> 3. "Then He will become despised (*i.e.* by the
> nations), and will cut off the glory of all the king-
> doms; they (Israel) will be prostrate and mourning,
> like a man of pains and like one destined to sick-
> ness; and as though the presence of the Shekhinah
> had been withdrawn from us, they will be despised,
> and esteemed not.

> 4. "Then for our sins He will pray, and our
> iniquities will for His sake be forgiven, although *we*
> were accounted stricken, smitten from before the
> Lord, and afflicted."

The Targum pictures the Messiah as a man of an

imposing, holy and awe-inspiring appearance (ver. 2). He
makes intercession for the sins of His people, and they
are forgiven for His sake (vers. 4, 6, 11, 12). His
prayers are answered, and before opening His mouth He
is accepted (v. 7). He is a great teacher. By His
wisdom He holds the guilty free from guilt, makes the
rebellious subject to the Law (vers. 11, 12); by His in-
struction peace increases upon His people, and on account
of its devotion to His words it obtains forgiveness of
sin (ver. 5). From subjection to the nations, from
chastisement and punishment, He delivers the souls of His
people (vers. 8, 11), builds the Holy Place (ver. 5), and
wondrous things are done to Israel in His days (ver. 8).
He overthrows the kingdoms of the nations (ver. 3),
scatters many peoples (ver. 15), the mighty of the peoples
He delivers like sheep to the slaughter (ver. 7), causes
the dominion of the Gentiles to pass away from the land
of Israel, and transfers on them the sins Israel had
committed (ver. 8), Israel looking on the punishment of
those that hated her, and is satisfied with the spoils of
their kings (ver. 11). But the Messiah is also judge of
His own people. He delivers the wicked to Gehenna,
and those who are rich in possessions into the death of
utter destruction (ver. 9).

With the advent of the Messiah a glorious time dawns
for Israel. The purified remnant looks on the kingdom
of the Messiah, their sons and daughters multiply, they
prolong their days, and those who perform the Law of
the Lord prosper in His good pleasure (ver. 10). The

10

righteous grow up before Him like blooming shoots, and like a tree which sends forth its roots to streams of water they increase—a holy generation in the land that was in need of Him (ver. 2).

Thus the Targum succeeded in reading into this chapter the whole Jewish Messianic hope, in which there was no place for a suffering Messiah. The words, "because He delivered up His soul to death," in verse 12, do not mean that the Messiah actually died, but rather, that He for the sake of His people, like Moses of old, was ready to give His life.

But the Targum, in spite of the high esteem in which it was held, found no imitators. Its method was too drastic, and the violence done to the sacred text too apparent to be imitated. We find, therefore, in early Rabbinic literature not a few passages which speak of a suffering Messiah; but they all belong to the time after the Mishna was edited, *i.e.* after 200 A.D.

THE TALMUD

1. THE NAME OF THE MESSIAH

In the Bab. Talmud, Sanhedrin 98^b, we read: "The Messiah—what is His name? . . . The Rabbis say, The leprous one of the house of Rabbi is His name, as it is said, 'Surely He hath borne our griefs . . . yet we did esteem Him stricken, smitten of God, and afflicted.'" The name, "The leprous one of the house of Rabbi," is very obscure. Dr. Pusey [1] has called attention to the better reading of this passage found in the *Pugio Fidei* by Raymundus Martini, where it reads: "The Rabbis say, The leprous one is His name; those of the house of Rabbi say, The sick one is His name," etc. In Isa. liii. 4 the word "stricken" [*nagua'*] is taken by the Rabbis as meaning stricken with leprosy, hence they give the name, "The leprous one." The house of Rabbi (*i.e.* R. Jehuda the saint, the editor of the Mishna) based their name, "The sick one," on the words "our griefs," lit. our diseases, having in mind their teacher, R. Jehuda, who had voluntarily taken upon himself bodily sufferings for thirteen years for the sake of the whole people, for during this period no pregnant woman died, nor did any miscarriage take place. [2]

2. B. Sanhedr. 93^b: "It is written (in Isa. xi. 3), And His delight (*haricho*) shall be in the fear of the Lord. R. Alexandri said, This indicates that He (God) will load Him (*i.e.* the Messiah) with commandments and sufferings as with millstones (*rechayim*)." It is not said here for what purpose the many sufferings will be laid on the Messiah, but the idea of a suffering Messiah is here expressed, although it has no connection with the Scripture quoted.

---

[1] *Cf.* The 53rd chapter of Isaiah, according to the Jewish interpreters, vol. ii. *Translations*, p. 34. The Jewish scholar, A. Epstein, in his *M'kadmonioth Ha-yehudim*, p. 109, defends Martini's reading.

[2] *Cf.* Jer. Talmud, Kil'ayim 32^b and Kethuboth 35^a.

3. B. Sanhedr. 98ᵃ.   Here we read: " R. Joshua, the
son of Levi (third cent. A.D.), met Elijah standing at
the door of the cave of R. Simeon ben Yochai. . . .
He said to him: When shall the Messiah come?   He
answered: Go and ask Him personally.—And where
does He abide?—At the gate of Rome.—And what is
His sign?—He abides among the poor who are stricken
by disease.   And all unbind, and bind up again, the
wounds at the same time, but He undoes (viz. the
bandage) and rebinds each separately, saying: Perhaps
I am wanted, and I would not be detained.   He went
to meet Him and said: Peace be to Thee, my Master
and my Teacher.   He replied to him: Peace be to
thee, son of Levi.   He said to Him: When wilt Thou
come, my Lord?   To-day, He replied.   Then he
returned to Elijah, who said unto him: What has He
said unto thee?   He said to me: Son of Levi, peace
be unto thee.   Elijah said unto him: He has assured
thee and thy father of the world to come.   He said
unto him: But He has deceived me in that He said:
I come to-day, and He has not come.   Elijah answered
him: It was so He meant—'To-day, if you will hear
My voice.' "

To understand this legend one must remember that,
according to the Rabbis, Messiah was born on the very
day Jerusalem was destroyed, and is now living in
obscurity.   According to this passage His place is at
the gate of Rome where He, though suffering, is waiting
every moment to be called to deliver His people.

THE MIDRASHIM

4. In Ruth Rabba 5, 6 (on ch. ii. 14) we read:
"'Come hither'—this refers to the King Messiah.
'Come hither,' draw near to the kingdom; 'and eat
of the bread,' that is, the bread of the kingdom; 'and
dip thy morsel in the vinegar,' this refers to the
sufferings, as it is said, 'But He was wounded for
our transgressions, bruised for our iniquities.'"

5. Midrash Tehillim on Ps. ii., and Midrash Samuel
ch. xix. (with the readings of the Yalkut, ii. 620):
"R. Hunā in the name of R. Achā says: The sufferings are divided into three parts: one for David and
the fathers, one for our own generation, and one for
the King Messiah, and this is what is written, 'He was
wounded for our transgressions,' etc. And when the
hour comes, says the Holy One—blessed be He!—to
them: I must create Him a new creation, as even it is
said, 'This day have I begotten thee.' This is the
hour when He is made a new creation."—So many and
great are Messiah's sufferings and afflictions that God
must create for Him a new body. It is not said in
what way, perhaps by raising Him from the dead.
Psalm ii. 7 is here used almost in the same way as it is
used by the Apostle Paul in Acts xiii. 33.

6. Pesiktha Rabbathi, chs. xxxiii.–xxxviii.[1] Nowhere
in Rabbinic literature are the sufferings of the Messiah
so graphically described and so expressly stated that

---

[1] Friedmann's edition, Vienna, 1880.

He is suffering for the sins of His people as in this Midrash. Apart from this, we have here a vague conception of the pre-existence of the Messiah, for the transaction between God and Messiah takes place at the beginning of creation, when man was not yet created.

Chapter xxxvi. is based on Isa. lx. 1, 2. Ps. xxxvi. 10 is quoted, and the question is asked, "What mean the words, *In thy light we see light*?"

"Which light is the congregation of Israel looking for? This is the light of Messiah, as it is written: And God saw the light, that it was good. This is intended to teach us, that the Holy One—blessed be He!—foresaw the Messiah and His works before the world was yet created, and He hid the light for the Messiah and His generation under His throne of glory. Said Satan before the Holy One—blessed be He!—Lord of the world, the light hidden under Thy throne of glory—for whom is it prepared? And He said to him: For Him who in the future will conquer thee, and cover thy face with shame. Said he: Lord of the world, show Him to me. Come and see, was the Divine answer; and when he saw Him, he began to tremble, and fell on his face, saying: Surely, this is Messiah, who in the future shall cast me and the (angelic) princes of the nations of the world into Gehenna, according to Isa. xxv. 8. . . ."

Messiah's Willingness to suffer for His People

"And the Holy One began to make an agreement with Him, saying, Those who are hidden with Thee— their sins will cause Thee to be put under an iron yoke, and they will make Thee like this calf whose eyes are dim, and they will choke Thy spirit under the yoke, and on account of their sins Thy tongue shall cleave to Thy mouth. Art Thou willing to do this? Said Messiah before the Holy One: Perhaps this anguish will last many years? And the Holy One said to Him: By Thy life, and by the life of My head, one week only have I decreed for Thee; but if Thy soul is grieved I shall destroy them even now. But He said to Him: Lord of all the worlds, with the gladness of My soul and the joy of My heart I take it upon Me, on condition that not one of Israel shall perish, and not only those alone should be saved who are in My days, but also those who are hid in the dust; and not only should the dead be saved who are in My days, but also those who have died from the days of the first Adam till now; and not only those, but also those who have been prematurely born. And not only those, but also those whom Thou hast intended to create, but who have not yet been created. Thus I agree, and thus I take all upon Me. In that hour the Holy One—blessed be He!—orders for Him four creatures to carry the throne of glory of the Messiah."

The Sufferings of the Messiah

"In the week when the Son of David comes, they bring beams of iron and put them (like a yoke) on His neck, until His stature is bent down. But He cries and weeps, and His voice ascends on high, and He says before Him: Lord of the world, what is My strength, the strength of My spirit, of My soul and of My members? Am I not flesh and blood? In view of that hour David wept, saying: 'My strength is dried up like a potsherd.'[1] In that hour the Holy One—blessed be He!—says to Him: Ephraim,[2] My righteous Messiah, Thou hast already taken this upon Thee from the six days of creation, now Thy anguish shall be like My anguish, for from the time that Nebuchadnezzar, the wicked one, has come and destroyed My house, and burned My Sanctuary, and sent My children into exile among the nations of the world, by Thy life and the life of My

---

[1] Ps. xxii. 16. Here the Editor has a note in which he calls attention to the fact that this psalm deals with the exile of the congregation of Israel, the sufferings of the Messiah and the future redemption, and that only on account of "the seditious talk of the heretics" (*i.e.* the Christians) the Rabbis explained it as referring to Esther.

[2] The Messiah is in these chapters called Ephraim, but not the Messiah, the son of Joseph, is here meant, as Dr. Edersheim thinks, but the Son of David, as can be seen from the words with which the passage begins (viz., "In the week when the Son of David comes"). I believe that they called the Messiah Ephraim on account of Jer. xxxi. 20, which passage they applied to the Messiah.

head, I have not sat down upon My throne. And if Thou wilt not believe Me, see the dew which is on My head, as it is said: 'My head is filled with dew.'[1] In that hour the Messiah answers Him: Lord of the world, now I am quited, *for it is enough for the servant that He is as His Master.*"[2]

Chapter xxxvii. describes Messiah's triumph and the glory which He receives as a due reward for His humiliation and sufferings on behalf of Israel. It is based on Isa. lxi. 10.

"The fathers of the world (the patriarchs) will rise again in the month of Nisan and will say to Him: Ephraim, our righteous Messiah, though we are Thy fathers, yet Thou art greater than we, because Thou hast borne the sins of our sons, and hard and evil measure has passed upon Thee, such as has not been passed either upon those before or upon those after. And Thou hast been for laughter and derision to the nations for the sake of Israel, and Thou hast dwelt in darkness and in gloominess, and Thine eyes have not seen light, and Thy skin was cleaving to Thy bones, and Thy body was as dry as wood, and Thine eyes were darkened through fasting, and Thy strength was dried up like a potsherd. And all this on account of the sins of our children. Is it Thy pleasure that our sons should enjoy the good things which the Holy One—blessed be He!—has poured out so abundantly upon Israel? Or, perhaps, on account of the anguish which Thou hast

---

[1] Cant. v. 2.   [2] pp. 161, 162.

suffered so much for them, and because they have chained Thee in the prison-house,[1] perhaps Thou art not pleased with them?

"Says He to them: Fathers of the world, whatever I have done I have only done for your sakes, and for the sake of your children, for the sake of your honour and that of your children, that they may enjoy the goodness which the Holy One—blessed be He!—has poured out over Israel. Then say to Him, the fathers of the world: Ephraim, our righteous Messiah, let Thy mind be at rest, as Thou hast put the mind of Thy Maker at rest and also our mind."

Messiah's Glory

"R. Simeon, the son of Pasi, said: In that hour the Holy One—blessed be He!—exalts the Messiah to the heaven of heavens, and spreads over Him the splendour of His glory. . . . And at once He makes for the Messiah seven canopies of precious stones and pearls. And from each canopy issue four streams of wine, honey, milk, and pure balsam. And the Holy One—blessed be He!—embraces Him in the presence of all the righteous ones and conducts Him into the Sanctuary,[2] and all the righteous ones see Him. And the Holy One

---

[1] This would indicate that He also suffered at the hand of His own people.

[2] The word "chuppah," canopy, means here the "seat of the Divine Majesty, Sanctuary." See Jastrow, *Talmudical Dictionary*, i. 437.

says unto them: Ye righteous ones of the world, Ephraim, the Messiah of My righteousness, has not yet received even the half for all He had suffered. But I have still one reward with Me which I will give unto Him, which no eye hath ever seen. In that hour the Holy One commands the North wind and the South wind, saying unto them: 'Come ye, and do honour and lie down before Ephraim, My righteous Messiah, fully loaded with all the perfumes from the Garden of Eden,' as it is said: 'Awake, O North wind; and come, thou South: blow upon My garden, that the spices thereof may flow out. Let My Beloved come into His garden, and eat His precious fruits.'"[1]

A MESSIANIC HYMN

" As a bridegroom decketh himself with a garland."[2]

"This teaches us that the Holy One shall clothe Ephraim, our righteous Messiah, with a garment, the splendour of which will be seen from one end of the world to the other end. And Israel shall walk in His light and say:

"Blessed is the hour when the Messiah was created!
Blessed the womb out of which He has come!
Blessed the generation whose eyes behold Him!
Blessed the eye that was waiting for Him!
For the opening of His lips is blessing and peace;
His whisper—a spiritual delight.
The thoughts of His heart are confidence and cheerfulness;
The speech of His tongue is pardon and forgiveness unto Israel.

[1] Cant. iv. 16, pp. 162*b*, 163*a*.   [2] Isa. lxi. 10.

His prayer is the sweet incense of offerings ;
His petitions are purity and holiness :
Blessed are His fathers who obtained the eternal good hidden
for ever !"[1]

THE LITURGY

The following remarkable hymn, by the famous hymn-writer, Eleazar ben Qualir, who, according to the Jewish historian, Zunz, lived in the ninth century A.D., is taken from the Service for the Day of Atonement.[2] In it are gathered up the teachings of the Synagogue about a suffering Messiah.

"Before the world was yet created,
    His dwelling-place and Yinnon[3] God prepared.
The Mount of His house, lofty from the beginning,
    He established, ere people and language existed.
It was His pleasure that there His Shekhina should dwell,
    To guide those gone astray into the path of rectitude.
Though their sins were red like scarlet,
    They were preceded by 'Wash you, make you clean.'
If His anger was kindled against His people,
    Yet the Holy One poured not out all His wrath.
We are ever threatened by destruction because of our evil deeds,
    And God does not draw nigh us—He, our only refuge.
Our righteous Messiah has departed from us,
    We are horror-stricken, and have none to justify us.

---

[1] p. 164*a*. See also Pesiktha d'rab Cahana, ed. Buber, p. 149, where the same hymn is quoted. There, however, the last line reads : "Blessed is Israel, for whom such has been prepared."

[2] *Cf.* The Festival Prayers, with David Levi's English translation, vol. iii. p. 33. The translation has been revised by me.

[3] "Yinnon" is, according to Bab. Sanhedrin 98*b*, one of Messiah's names according to Ps. lxxii. 17, which the Talmud renders, "Before the Sun, Yinnon (Heb., shall flourish) was His name," the name indicating the pre-existence of the Messiah.

Our iniquities and the yoke of our transgressions
  He carries who is wounded because of our transgressions.
He bears on His shoulder the burden of our sins,
  To find pardon for all our iniquities.
By His stripes we shall be healed—
  O Eternal One, it is time that thou shouldst create Him
    anew !
O bring Him up from the terrestrial sphere,
  Raise Him up from the land of Seir,[1]
To announce salvation to us from Mount Lebanon,[2]
  Once again through the hand of Yinnon."

THE ZOHAR (VOL. II. 212*a*)

"The souls which are in the garden of Eden below go to and fro every new moon and Sabbath, in order to ascend to the place that is called the Walls of Jerusalem. . . . After that they journey on and contemplate all those that are possessed of pains and sicknesses and those that are martyrs for the unity of their Lord, and then return and announce it to the Messiah. And as they tell Him of the misery of Israel in their captivity, and of those wicked ones among them who are not attentive to know their Lord, He lifts up His voice and weeps for their wickedness: and so it is written, 'He was wounded for our transgressions,' etc. Then those souls return and abide in their own place.

---

[1] Seir stands here for Edom, and by Edom the Talmud means Rome, where, as we have seen above, the Messiah already lives in deep humiliation and suffering.

[2] Lebanon stands here for the Mount of the Temple, from which Messiah is to proclaim to Israel that the time of salvation has come.

"There is in the garden of Eden a palace called the palace of the sons of sickness: this palace the Messiah then enters, and summons every sickness, every pain, and every chastisement of Israel; they all come and rest upon Him. And were it not that He had thus lightened them off Israel and taken them upon Himself, there had been no man able to bear Israel's chastisements for transgression of the law: and this is that which is written, 'Surely our sicknesses He hath carried.'"[1]

---

[1] The Zohar, the Bible of the Mystics, contains another tradition about the concealed existence of the Messiah preceding His Advent. He lives in Paradise, in a place called The Bird's Nest (Kān Tsippor), from whence He will appear to save Israel. *Cf.* Zohar, II. 7*b*.